MIRACLE in ETHIOPIA

MIRACLE IN ETHIOPIA

a partnership response to famine

Richard W. Solberg

FRIENDSHIP PRESS • NEW YORK

Copyright © 1991 by Friendship Press
Editorial Offices:
475 Riverside Drive, New York, NY 10115
Distribution Offices:
P.O. Box 37844, Cincinnati, OH 45222-0844

Manufactured in the United States of America

Library of Congress Cataloging in Publication Data

Solberg, Richard W., 1917–
   Miracle in Ethiopia : a partnership response to famine / Richard
W. Solberg.
     p.   cm.
   Includes bibliographical references and index.
   ISBN 0-377-00215-1
   1. Food relief, American—Ethiopia. 2. Famines—Ethiopia.
3. Church charities—United States. 4. Church charities—Ethiopia.
I. Title.
HV696.F6S64   1991
363.8'83'0963—dc20   90-49116
                                         CIP

Contents

MAPS

PHOTOS

Preface ————————————————

MILLIONS OF PERSONS who witnessed on television the horror scenes from Ethiopian starvation camps in October 1984, would have, in all honesty, described their experience as "unforgettable." Rarely, if ever, have the grim realities of famine been so graphically brought before the eyes of the world. Never has such a spontaneous wave of compassion swept across the Western world as that which arose in response to those pictures. But six years have passed since then. The tragedies of Armenia, Bangladesh, Sudan, and Beijing have appeared in succession in full color on the same TV screens, and "unforgettable" has become a relative term.

It has not been my intention in the pages that follow to attempt a re-creation of those scenes so compellingly captured on film in 1984. I have sought instead to describe a "miracle in Ethiopia," the compassionate response that saved millions of lives and built new bridges of human understanding between people and institutions. I have tried to answer the question that has been asked again and again by friends and critics alike: "Did the food sent to feed the starving really reach those who needed it?" The question will be answered with an emphatic "Yes."

The story also tells of the incredible complexities inherent in an international relief effort in a country without an adequate internal transport system, economically and spiritually drained by twenty-eight years of civil war, and la-

boring under a government more concerned with ideology
than with the welfare of its people. It will recognize the
contributions of a worldwide network of churches, agencies, and individuals who sent money and medical supplies to relieve the suffering people of Ethiopia. And it will
acknowledge the overwhelming generosity of governments,
especially that of the United States, which, under persistent pressure by the Congress and the American people, finally placed human welfare above ideology and contributed
one-third of the world total of emergency food entering
Ethiopia.

The book describes one among the many private responses to the Ethiopian famine, by an international partnership of Lutherans and Roman Catholics, working hand in
hand with their counterpart churches in Ethiopia. By far the
largest of the private relief programs in Ethiopia, the Joint
Relief Partnership was responsible for distributing one-fourth
of the total tonnage of relief food brought into Ethiopia from
1984 to 1986.

In the early part of the account that follows, the partnership operated under the name of Churches Drought Action
Africa/Ethiopia, or CDAA/E. In December 1985, the name
was changed to the Joint Relief Partnership (JRP) to distinguish it from a similarly-named consortium of agencies in
Geneva, Switzerland.

Not long thereafter, another manifestation of the "miracle" occurred. The Ethiopian Orthodox Church, the majority
Christian communion in Ethiopia, with more than 20 million
members, became a full member of the JRP, thus uniting for
the first time in fifteen hundred years the entire Christian
community of Ethiopia in the biblically mandated mission of
feeding the hungry.

It was in part their gratitude for this ecumenical gift that
motivated the executives of the JRP to sponsor this history
of their joint endeavor. They were also eager that the risks
and sacrifices willingly undertaken by the hundreds of workers who became partners with those they served be documented, and that their common experiences, both successes

and failures, might be helpful to others in meeting future crises.

Many persons and institutions have made significant contributions toward the fulfillment of their intent. Administration of the project was delegated by the partners to Catholic Relief Services (CRS), then in New York City. Claire McCurdy, CRS Archivist, prepared the prospectus, conducted the initial survey of resources, and directed the project until February 1989. Sister Rosalie McQuaide succeeded McCurdy and shepherded the project to completion. Peter Schaufele assisted in organizing and microfilming the collected documents.

In addition to the CRS archives in New York, documentary sources were provided by Lutheran World Relief, New York City; the archives of the Evangelical Lutheran Church in America, Chicago; offices of CRS and Lutheran World Federation in Geneva, Switzerland; and Caritas Internationalis in Rome. In Addis Ababa documentary resources were made available by the secretariat of the Joint Relief Partnership, by Catholic Relief Services, Lutheran World Federation, the Ethiopian Evangelical Church Mekane Yesus, and the Ethiopian Catholic Secretariat; and also by the U.S. Embassy and the Institute of Ethiopian Studies at the University of Addis Ababa.

Among the most valuable contributions were more than fifty recorded oral history interviews with persons who played prominent roles in JRP operations in Ethiopia, Europe, and the United States. Insights provided by these persons left no doubt concerning the spirit and commitment that motivated the program of the JRP.

Valuable comments and suggestions were made by staff members of the partnership churches and agencies and by Carl Solberg, who read the entire manuscript. Mary Solberg edited the final version.

Special thanks and commendation are reserved for research associate and editorial consultant June N. Solberg. She collaborated in conducting oral history interviews and transcribed most of the tapes. As the manuscript developed,

she transferred the author's handwritten pages to the word
processor and patiently typed dozens of re-edited versions.
She also prepared the index. Most of all, her personal commitment to this task has been for the author an indispens-
able source of support and encouragement. In every sense,
this book is the product of a partnership.

RICHARD W. SOLBERG

Thousand Oaks, California

Abbreviations ————————————

AID	Agency for International Development
CDAA	Churches Drought Action Africa
CDAA/E	Churches Drought Action Africa/Ethiopia
CI	Caritas Internationalis
CICARWS	Commission on Inter-Church Aid, Refugee and World Service, World Council of Churches
CRDA	Christian Relief and Development Association
CRS	Catholic Relief Services
CWS	Church World Service
DICAD	Department of Interchurch Aid and Development, Ethiopian Orthodox Church
ECE	Evangelical Church of Eritrea
ECS	Ethiopian Catholic Secretariat
ECU	European Currency Unit
EEC	European Economic Community
EECMY	Ethiopian Evangelical Church Mekane Yesus
EOC	Ethiopian Orthodox Church
ICRC	International Committee of the Red Cross

ICRHA	Interchurch Response for the Horn of Africa
JCAFR	Joint Church Action for Famine Relief
JRP	Joint Relief Partnership
LWF	Lutheran World Federation
LWR	Lutheran World Relief
NATRACO	National Transport Corporation
NGO	Non-Governmental Organization
OFDA	Office for Foreign Disaster Assistance
PVO	Private Voluntary Organization
RRC	Relief and Rehabilitation Commission, Government of Ethiopia
UNDRO	United Nations Disaster Relief Organization
USAID	U.S. Agency for International Development
WCC	World Council of Churches
WFP	World Food Program
WHO	World Health Organization
WV	World Vision

E T H I O P I A

SAUDI ARABIA

RED SEA

ERITREA

SUDAN

Massawa

Asmara

Aksum   Adwa

TIGRAY

GONDAR

Makelle

Lake Tana   Korem

Ibenat   Kobo

WOLLO   Danaki   YEMEN

Desert

Assab

DJIBOUTI

GULF OF ADEN

GOJJAM   Kombolcha   Bati

Blue   Dessie

Nile

WOLLEGA   Addis Ababa   Dire Dawa

Nazareth

SHOA   HARARGE

ILUBABOR   ARSI

KAFFA   Ogaden

GAMO   BALE

GOFA

SIDAMO

AFRICA

KENYA

SOMALIA

SCALE OF MILES
0   50   100   200   300

SCALE OF KILOMETERS
0   50 100   200   300

– – – – – –   provincial borders

————————   main highways

++++++++   railroad

MIRACLE *in* ETHIOPIA

"This disaster had not struck without warning. Records reaching back a thousand years record Ethiopian famines recurring in dreary sequence, with death tolls reaching the hundreds of thousands."

"The reluctance of both the United States and the European community to offer even emergency aid to the people of a Marxist-led country contributed to the deaths of hundreds of thousands of people."

I

Raising the Curtain ─────────

ON THE MORNING of November 12, 1984, a small convoy of Land Rovers wound its way out of Addis Ababa, Ethiopia's capital city, and headed northward to the famine-stricken provinces of Wollo and Tigray. Laden with cameras and microphones rather than grain and milk, this was the television crew for CBS's "60 Minutes." A week later, on November 18, thousands of American families would get their first look at the heart-wrenching scenes of starvation in the crowded camps of Bati and Makelle.

They would watch as a baby born to a starving mother in a dirty lane outside the camp shelters was cradled in a paper sack to protect it from the swirling dust. They would be told that in the camp of 25,000 refugees at Bati there were only three nurses and one doctor. They would visit a room that sheltered 50 babies, but where no crying was heard because the infants, needing all their energy for the next breath, didn't have enough strength to cry. Fifty bodies a day were being buried. One person observed that those being buried might well be called the lucky ones.

Accompanying correspondent Mike Wallace as guide and adviser was an American Catholic priest, Monsignor Robert Coll, the newly appointed coordinator of Churches Drought Action Africa/Ethiopia (CDAA/E). This ecumenical venture, recently organized by Catholic and Protestant churches and

international agencies, would acquire and distribute emergency food donated for the relief of these victims of disaster.

Mike Wallace's pilgrimage to Bati and Makelle was only
one of many efforts to capitalize on what Kenyan journalist Mohammed Amin's news footage, broadcast three weeks
earlier on the BBC, had transformed into a gripping story,
aptly titled "African Calvary." Monsignor Coll, on the other
hand, was representative of churches, agencies, and individuals who had already been battling the Ethiopian famine for
two years and trying — perhaps not eloquently enough —
to awaken governments and the world at large on behalf of
millions of voiceless, starving people.

Partners in Compassion

Each member of the CDAA/E had been involved in Ethiopia
for many years. The two indigenous partners, the Ethiopian Roman Catholic Church and the Ethiopian Evangelical Church Mekane Yesus, a Lutheran body, maintained
long-established parishes, institutions, development projects,
and relief operations throughout the country. The other
two partners were international organizations. Catholic Relief Services (CRS), an American-based international relief
and development agency of the United States Catholic Conference, was also a member of Caritas Internationalis (CI),
the worldwide network of Catholic relief and development
agencies, active in 118 countries. The Lutheran World Federation (LWF), an association of over 100 Lutheran church
bodies in 93 countries, maintained aid programs in 50 countries through its Department of World Service.

When governments of the world finally made available
large amounts of emergency food for distribution, these indigenous churches and their counterpart international agencies, already equipped with an extensive infrastructure, stood
ready to serve. They had the advantage of a history of providing social services, and personnel familiar with the country, its needs, and its people. Other foreign-based agencies

had to bring in large numbers of expatriates and establish new centers for the distribution of food.

Between 1984 and 1986, the CDAA/E partnership was responsible for delivering a total of 428,000 metric tons* of food, 25 percent of all relief food distributed, making it the largest nongovernmental supplier of emergency food. While it is impossible to know how many lives were saved through its efforts, the number of *daily* beneficiaries of the CDAA/E food programs was estimated at more than two million.

Monsignor Coll's questions during his "60 Minutes" interview with Mike Wallace were more than rhetorical. Why, he asked, had world response to this monumental tragedy been so slow? Why had this catastrophe been allowed to reach such devastating proportions before the world responded? Had there been no warnings? Were no resources available? The United States Congress had long ago passed legislation reflecting the desires of the American people to feed the world's poor. The European Economic Community (EEC) had regular channels for providing emergency aid. Yet in both the United States and in Europe mountainous surpluses overflowed storage facilities. Long-term storage cost more than it would have cost to provide the grain at cost to Ethiopia or other famine-threatened countries of Africa. There was little doubt that Western governments were reluctant to assist a country like Ethiopia whose leaders were avowed Marxists. "People who link politics and food in this way," declared Monsignor Coll, "are executioners."[1]

This disaster had not struck without warning. Records reaching back a thousand years record famines recurring in dreary sequence, with death tolls reaching the hundreds of thousands. The most recent one, less than a decade earlier, had contributed to toppling Emperor Haile Selassie. Students and the military rose in arms, refusing to allow a curtain of silence to cover the cries of the dying.

When the rains again began to fail in the early 1980s, those who remembered the catastrophe of 1972–73 sounded

*Hereafter identified as "tons." One metric ton equals 2,200 pounds.

the warning. The Relief and Rehabilitation Commission (RRC), established by the Ethiopian government in 1974 to monitor agricultural conditions and prospects for annual harvests, publicized the mounting shortages of food. The Protestant and Catholic churches of Ethiopia and their international partners alerted their constituencies and called for immediate support. Traveling journalists who were able to gain access to the country supported these appeals. In June 1983 Jay Ross of the *Washington Post* described the famine in graphic detail and deplored the U.S. government's lack of response. Few reporters, however, got into Ethiopia and even fewer were permitted to visit the stricken areas.

A Case of Public Apathy

Ten years earlier, in the fall of 1973, television had assisted in unmasking an Ethiopian famine. British reporter Jonathan Dimbleby's film "The Unknown Famine" was credited with inciting outrage that resulted in the overthrow of Emperor Haile Selassie. On the night they deposed him, his captors forced the old emperor to view this footage before he was hustled away in a dilapidated Volkswagen, never to be seen in public again.[2]

But in 1983–84 television's apathy and ignorance were actually part of the problem. In the summer of 1983 CBS commissioned an American free-lance producer to prepare a film on the Ethiopian famine. But when he returned to New York with his product, he was told the images were not strong enough — not enough people were caught in the act of dying. Another photographer, Anthony Suau, assisted by CRS, brought back a series of pictures that were rejected by his editor on the same grounds. A year later they won a Pulitzer prize.[3]

What could account for this initial lack of response from media, from governments, from fellow human beings basking in one of the most prosperous and well-fed decades of modern history? Part of the reason was probably the ineffectiveness of the information networks of relief agencies that possessed the tragic facts and made diligent efforts to report them. Church press, government reports, and field observations reach limited audiences. They have even less impact when they deal with obscure places and relatively unknown people. The traditional Western image of African countries as mostly undeveloped, politically chaotic, and chronically poor has placed African concerns low on Western scales of priorities. In 1984, when the horrors of the Ethiopian famine were finally revealed, large numbers of people were not even able to locate Ethiopia on a map.

Causes deserving of human response seemed to be multiplying daily. Hunger, homelessness, natural disaster, refugees, relief, and rehabilitation were placing unprecedented demands on both private agencies and governments. In the early 1980s Ethiopia itself was only one manifestation of the disaster that threatened the entire sub-Saharan belt of nations where the wind and sand of the encroaching desert were steadily reducing productive fields to wasteland. To which major disaster area of the world should the resources of compassionate human beings be directed?

In fact, the magnitude of the Ethiopian crisis extended far beyond the capacities of private individuals or agencies. National governments and international agencies had to be enlisted. Deployment of these powerful instruments of relief, however, was restrained as political concerns took precedence over humane considerations. The reluctance of both the United States and the European community to offer even emergency aid to the people of a Marxist-led country, until they were forced by public pressure, contributed to the death of hundreds of thousands of people.

More reprehensible, because it violated the trust and well-being of its own citizens, the Ethiopian government refused to acknowledge the disastrous famine among its own people. In spite of the nearly ten years of warnings issued by its own Relief and Rehabilitation Commission, the Marxist head of state, Lt. Col. Mengistu Haile Mariam, directed national resources to the building of a military establishment to combat the rebel insurgency in the provinces of Eritrea and Tigray. Most shocking of all was the massive government expenditure during 1984 in preparation for the tenth anniversary of the Revolution in September, while thousands of peasants in the provinces were dying of starvation.[4]

No "Quick Fix"

The famine that devastated Ethiopia in 1984–85 and shocked the Western world was by no means a one-time event in Ethiopian experience. It did not happen because of unique circumstances that, if expeditiously handled, would not happen again. The conditions so vividly depicted on television were not subject to a "quick fix."

Famines build gradually. A single year or even several years of drought may result in hunger and deprivation, but do not necessarily produce a famine. Famine finally grips a nation only when the national structures fail to acknowledge food shortages and deal irresponsibly with available supplies for the people. It comes with the final failure of rains that might have nourished the last seeds purchased by the sale of household goods, family heirlooms, tools, and livestock.

Famine comes to individual families when their last resources have literally been consumed. Starvation — the final link in this chain of death — comes at last only to individual persons.

Such were the hopeless prospects that triggered the mournful mass movements toward roads and towns, in whatever direction rumor suggested food might be found. The survivors of these death marches crowded into the camps at Bati and Makelle, and by means of television, into the comfortable living rooms of Europe and America.

"The golden age of Ethiopian history may well have been the brilliant but little-known epic of the Kingdom of Aksum, beginning in the first century of the Christian era."

"Despite the Marxist allegiance of the present government, the religious tradition is still the most profound expression of the Ethiopian national ethos. Christianity claims over one-half and Muslims account for about one-third of the population."

II

A Profile of the Land ————————

AMONG THE FIRST EUROPEANS to explore the western coast
of Africa in the fifteenth century and to venture into the
Indian Ocean beyond the Cape of Good Hope, Portuguese
sailors were haunted by the legend of a Christian king
called "Prester John," who ruled a vast and wealthy kingdom somewhere in Africa. Drawn by the lure of wealth or
the desire for a Christian ally against their Moslem rivals,
Portuguese sea captains from Vasco da Gama on dreamed of
finding this fabulous realm. Whether the ancient Abyssinian
kingdom we know as Ethiopia was indeed the land of
their dreams, it has retained even in modern times a semi-
mythical character.

Ethiopia, hidden among the lofty mountains and high
plateaus of the "horn of Africa," was the only country to sur-
vive the partition of Africa by imperialist Europe in the nineteenth century. The only African people to develop their own
written alphabet, still in use today, Ethiopians also maintain
the oldest unbroken Christian tradition of any nation in the
world.

Geographically, Ethiopia is the third largest country in
Africa, twice the size of France and equal in size to the states
of California, Arizona, New Mexico, and Utah. Its population
of 42 million is greater than that of Spain and exceeds that
of New York and California combined. Its terrain is among

11

the world's most rugged, dominated by a central highland plateau rising 6,000 to 10,000 feet above sea level. The country is bisected from northeast to southwest by the Great Rift Valley, one of the world's geological wonders, extending from Syria through the Red Sea and 4,000 miles south into the heart of Africa. Mountainous peaks tower 14–15,000 feet and descend into precipitous gorges, too steep even for pack animals. The Blue Nile rises in the fabled Lake Tana and winds 850 miles north and west to join the White Nile at Khartoum in neighboring Sudan. The vast Sahara desert on the west and the Ogaden and Danakil deserts and the Red Sea on the east provide the protective barriers that have helped to maintain the political and cultural integrity — and isolation — of this ancient inland empire.

Climatic conditions vary as dramatically as the topography. Lying as close to the equator as it does, Ethiopia might be expected to have a torrid tropical climate, as indeed it has along its eastern and western lowlands. Parts of the Danakil desert lie below sea level, receive virtually no rain, and are among the hottest places on earth. But much of the highland plateau, where the majority of the people live, enjoys a temperate climate and ordinarily is blessed with ample rainfall and moderate temperatures.

In the national capital, Addis Ababa, at an altitude of over 8,000 feet, the average temperature in May, the hottest month, is 65 degrees Fahrenheit, and in December, the coldest month, is 58 degrees. However, in the northern highlands of Wollo and Tigray, where the drought of 1984–86 was most severe, elevations rise to 10,000 feet and the climate is cool and windy. Near-freezing night-time temperatures in refugee camps intensified the misery of the thousands already suffering from hunger and starvation.[1]

From Solomon to Mengistu

The people of Ethiopia have an ancient and distinguished history. Tradition claims the establishment of the royal line by Emperor Menelik I, the son of King Solomon of Israel and Makeda, Queen of Sheba, nine hundred years before Christ. The late emperor Haile Selassie, who claimed to be the 225th descendant of this line, referred to himself as "the Lion of Judah and the King of Kings."

The golden age of Ethiopian history may well have been the brilliant but little-known epic of the Kingdom of Aksum. Beginning in the first century of the Christian era, this empire dominated the region of the Red Sea and southern Arabia for more than seven hundred years. During the height of Aksumite power in the fourth century C.E., King Ezana accepted the Christian faith and established Christianity as the official state religion of Ethiopia.

For more than a thousand years following the decline of the Aksumite kingdom, Ethiopian rulers fought to prevent the submergence of the empire and its religion by the expanding waves of Islam that swept the Near East and North Africa after the death of Mohammed in 632 C.E. Against formidable odds, but aided by the rugged terrain of their homeland, they were able to preserve their integrity against Islam and, later, against nineteenth century European colonialism. By the end of the last century Ethiopia emerged as the only remaining independent nation in Africa.

In the late nineteenth century Italy managed to gain a foothold on the Red Sea coast of Eritrea and even to carry out a brief invasion of the highlands. But in a historic battle at Adwa in 1896, the Ethiopian army of Menelik II soundly defeated the Italian invaders and drove them back to their bases in Eritrea on the Red Sea. In 1935, the Italian dictator Benito Mussolini successfully invaded Ethiopia and exiled Emperor Haile Selassie, but in 1941 British forces liberated the country and restored the emperor to his throne.

A decade later, dissent over the political status of Eritrea, the erstwhile Italian colony, broke out; in 1962 a civil war for Eritrean independence erupted. In 1974 a group of young military officers, later called the Dergue, led by Lt. Col. Mengistu Haile Mariam, overthrew Ethiopia's aging emperor. With the support of the Soviet Union, they established a Marxist state.

The civil war, now in its twenty-eighth year, continues, sapping the human and economic resources of the nation. Fighting is fiercest in Eritrea and Tigray, the areas most seriously affected by famine. Relief efforts have been consistently hampered and often interrupted.[2]

The people of Ethiopia represent a variety of ethnic and tribal groups and languages. The two largest tribal groups are the Oromo and the Amhara. Though fewer in number, the Amharas have been the dominant group, and their language has become the official language of the country. The general literacy level is only about 65 percent and literacy training and public education are energetically promoted by the government. Centered in the capital and in other larger towns and cities, a highly educated group supplies a competent civil service and active academic and business communities. The former emperor encouraged higher education, both by endowing a university in one of the imperial palaces in the capital and by encouraging overseas study by competent young Ethiopians. This process has enriched the cultural climate of both Ethiopia and the countries where many Ethiopians have elected to stay as permanent residents and citizens.

Ethiopia's Churches

Despite the Marxist allegiance of the present government, the religious tradition is still the most profound expression of the Ethiopian national ethos. Christianity claims over one-half and Muslims account for about one-third of the population. The vast majority of Christians are members of the Ethiopian Orthodox Church. Ethiopia probably counts more Christians among its 42 million people than any other country in Africa.

The Ethiopian Orthodox Church (EOC), headed by its patriarch and twenty-four archbishops and bishops, professes allegiance neither to Rome nor to any capital of Eastern Orthodoxy. Its independent stance dates from 451 C.E. when the church leaders of Alexandria refused to accept the dogma of the Council of Chalcedon concerning the two natures of Christ, a position the Ethiopian Orthodox Church continues to share with the Coptic Church of Egypt. Its 20,000 parishes are currently served by 250,000 clergy. The official ecclesiastical language used in liturgical worship is Ge'ez, the ancient classical language of Ethiopia. Like the Latin of the Roman Church, however, it is gradually being replaced by Amharic, the modern national language.

Until recent years neither education nor social concern has been emphasized by the EOC, either among clergy or laity. The recent establishment of a theological seminary and several clergy training centers reflects new directions for the Orthodox Church. Emergency relief activities are handled by the Church's Department of Interchurch Aid and Development (DICAD), established in 1965. Encouraged and aided by the World Council of Churches, the EOC has also undertaken responsible efforts to cooperate in alleviating famine. During the 1984–86 crisis the CDAA/E provided food for distribution through centers opened by DICAD, and in 1987 the EOC became a fully participating member of the Joint Relief Partnership (JRP).[3]

In terms of membership the Roman Catholic Church in Ethiopia is a small minority, claiming only about 330,000 adherents. Nevertheless, it has deep historical roots planted by the Portuguese as early as the sixteenth century. Jesuit missionaries accompanied the soldiers who came to Ethiopia's aid against the Muslims and remained in the country until a popular uprising forced their withdrawal in 1632. Catholic missionaries returned with the Italian invasion in the nineteenth century and during the Italian War of the 1930s made important gains, especially in Eritrea.

The Roman Catholic Church operates nine ecclesiastical districts in the country, with a cardinal archbishop resident in Addis Ababa. There are 541 diocesan and missionary priests and 350 seminarists. More than 900 sisters and lay brothers

serve in 88 charitable institutions and 161 parish schools and
other educational institutions. In 1965 the Episcopal Conference created the Ethiopian Catholic Secretariat (ECS) to
coordinate and improve educational, medical, social, and development activities of the church. As a participating member of Caritas Internationalis, the ECS was able to provide
emergency services during the famine of 1973–74 and now
represents the Catholic Church as a full partner in the Joint
Relief Partnership.[4]

Although it was instituted as a national church as recently as 1959, the Ethiopian Evangelical Church Mekane
Yesus (EECMY) represents the presence of an evangelical
movement in Ethiopia dating from the seventeenth century.
It began with the translation of portions of the New Testa-
ment into Amarigna (Amharic) by Peter Heyling (1607–52),
a German Lutheran who spent eighteen years at the royal
court in Gondar. In the early nineteenth century an Ethiopian monk in Cairo completed the translation of the entire
Bible, which, after its publication by the British and Foreign
Bible Society, inspired a spiritual revival among many Orthodox priests and led to the forming of evangelical associations
for the study of the Scriptures.

In 1854 and 1866 missionary societies in Germany and
Sweden undertook evangelistic efforts among the largely
non-Christian Oromo people in the western and southern
parts of Ethiopia.

Their work and that of later missionaries from other communions was not welcomed by the established Orthodox
Church and often resulted in persecution and even expulsion from the country. Following World War II a strong indigenous leadership led to the formation of local Ethiopian
evangelical congregations, and in 1959 to a national evangelical church.

The EECMY now numbers over 800,000 members, in
2140 congregations. It has 229 pastors and 1,000 lay evan-
gelists, and is organized in eight autonomous geographic
synods. It took the name Mekane Yesus, meaning "The
Place of Jesus," from the large congregation in Addis Ababa

that had given strong leadership in the process of organization.

In 1963 the EECMY became a member of the Lutheran
World Federation (LWF), and during the famine of 1973–74 it
first requested assistance from the LWF in meeting that emergency. Through its Department of Development the EECMY
conducts major projects of relief and rehabilitation and of
land and water conservation. Together with its international
counterpart, the LWF, the EECMY has been a full partner
in the founding and operation of the CDAA/E (now Joint
Relief Partnership).[5]

Economic Patterns and Problems

Ethiopia has an almost exclusively agricultural economy and
is one of the poorest countries in the world, with a per capita
annual income of $110 in 1985. Cattle, sheep, and a variety
of grains, especially a native crop called "teff," constitute major food resources. Coffee accounts for more than 60 percent
of the nation's exports, supplemented by a variety of miner-
als such as coal, gold, platinum, copper, and potash. Trade
is carried on through the two Red Sea ports of Massawa
and Assab, and through the former French colonial port of
Djibouti, now an independent nation. Ethiopia's only railroad connects Djibouti to Ethiopia's capital of Addis Ababa,
a city of about two million people located in the center of
the country.

As the distinguished British scholar on Ethiopia Richard
Pankhurst has documented, periodic drought in certain parts
of Ethiopia is probably endemic, reflecting both general climatic conditions and the peculiar topography of the country,
in which altitudes vary from sub-sea level to nearly 15,000
feet within relatively short distances.[6] Normally, there are
two periods of rainfall, an early period from February to
April, called the "belg" rains, and a later period, from July
to September, called the "kerempt" rains. Inconsistencies or
failures of either of these, especially the latter, heavier rains,

can produce serious crop shortages or even failures in one
part of the country or other. This was a major factor in the
drought of 1984–85, since several such recurrences had been
experienced, particularly in the northern provinces, over a
succession of years since 1980.

Other factors of long standing added to the severity of
the recent famine, as they had in previous disasters. Primitive farming methods, generations old, have contributed to
the deterioration and erosion of the soil and the decimation
of forests, especially on the steep hillsides of the northern
provinces. Deforestation has gradually denuded other once
heavily wooded areas elsewhere, further contributing to the
erosion of the soil. Peasants living on the chilly highlands,
8,000 to 10,000 feet above sea level, have heated their simple dwellings and cooked their meals with firewood for generations. A century ago about 44 percent of Ethiopia was
forested. By 1950 the forest area had been reduced to 16 percent. Today it is down to just 4 percent, most of which is in
the south. The north is virtually treeless.[7]

Rapid population growth has also contributed to the food
problem. In spite of an infant mortality rate of 115 per 1,000
live births and a nationwide life expectancy of only forty
years, the population continues to increase by 2.9 percent
per year. Ethiopia is now the third most populous country
in Africa, surpassed only by Nigeria and Egypt.

Nevertheless, a country as large and varied as Ethiopia,
which still possesses significant areas of fertile and arable
soil, could feed itself if it pursued an agricultural policy in-
tentionally directed toward food production. Instead, government policy has encouraged the production of cash crops
such as coffee and cotton for export to the Western world.
Low fixed prices for agricultural products benefiting urban
consumers at farmers' expense have tended to undermine the
initiative of farmers to produce food crops beyond their own
immediate needs.[8]

Weather patterns in Ethiopia will continue to be capri-
cious, resulting in periodic droughts. But recurrent famine
need not be its lot forever. Drought has become famine in

Ethiopia because of primitive and wasteful farming methods, misguided government agricultural policies, and civil war — factors largely subject to human remedy. Concerted efforts for rehabilitation and prevention can and must eventually replace massive relief programs like those of 1984–86.

"By 1985, forty-six voluntary agencies were operating their own relief programs in Ethiopia."

"A combination of apathy and politics would bring about almost fatal delays in gaining access to life-saving resources."

"Pressure exerted on the administration in Washington by members of Congress and by private voluntary agencies also resulted in the restoration to the budget of the regular nonemergency food program for Ethiopia."

III

The Impending Disaster ⸺

In a country where food shortages are normal, it is difficult to establish a specific point when hunger becomes acute rather than chronic. In the case of Ethiopia, by the time substantial help reached its people in late 1984 that point had long been passed. Thousands had literally starved to death. Signs of acute hunger were clearly evident in the highland provinces of Wollo and Tigray early in 1982. Had the regime in Addis Ababa and the governments of other countries around the world taken action then, the death camps of Korem and Bati that galvanized world opinion two and a half years later would not have existed.

Shortages first began to appear in the northern provinces, in the wake of poor harvests in 1980 and 1981, and several thousand farmers and their families fled from the central highlands to more fertile areas in the west. In April 1982, the Relief and Rehabilitation Commission (RRC) of the Ethiopian government stated that three million people were facing food shortages because of the failure of seasonal rains, and another two million because of the destructive civil war in the northern provinces. In the fall of 1982, when more than 400,000 peasants abandoned their farms and moved westward, it became clear that a major famine was at hand.

Shelters were set up by the government at Korem for 24,000 people and at Makelle for 30,000.[1]

In September 1982, on the initiative of the Christian Relief and Development Association (CRDA), a group established in 1974 to coordinate activities of private relief and development agencies in Ethiopia, a survey team including representatives of the EOC and CRS traveled to Tigray and Eritrea to assess needs and recommend possible relief measures. They reported vigorous efforts by local churches and by the RRC to set up shelters and to provide food and medical care for thousands of persons in and around Makelle, Aksum, and Adwa who had been displaced by crop failures and military activity. In one shelter in Makelle seven children had succumbed to whooping cough and meningitis. One member of the survey team concluded his report by observing, "I am sorry to state that the need is greater than the resources available. Therefore external assistance is needed to combat hunger in Ethiopia."[2]

Early Responses

Six months later, in March 1983, Father Stephanos Tedla, executive secretary of ECS in Addis Ababa, also made a survey trip to Korem in Wollo province. He reported crowds of famished people streaming into the government's camps and issued a call to all voluntary agencies, especially to the Catholic community of Ethiopia and the Caritas network in Rome, of which ECS was a member.[3]

Before the year was over, grain shipments began to arrive from Caritas/Germany and from the EEC. In May, ECS received 10,000 blankets and tents and 470 tons of food from Caritas/Germany. The Catholic churches in Asmara cooperated with the RRC in operating five shelters in the region. Brother Cesare Bullo, coordinator of the Catholic Social Action Committee in Tigray, one of the first to alert both CRS and ECS in Addis Ababa to the worsening crisis, received a shipment from Canada sufficient for two months' feeding, and a thousand blankets from ECS to shield from the cold winds at Makelle.[4]

The Evangelical Church Mekane Yesus (EECMY) and its international counterpart, the Lutheran World Federation (LWF), also launched a famine relief effort in 1983, much of it in the form of transportation of grain received by the RRC to points of special need. Recognizing that the most seriously affected areas were in the north, EECMY/LWF concentrated its aid in those provinces. As early as April 1983, it began work in Wollo, allocating $720,000 for transporting 6,000 tons of RRC grain. In Eritrea, it transported 1,500 tons of grain from the EEC, and provided $12,000 in medical supplies and 10,000 blankets for Barentu.[5]

An additional 4,500 tons contributed by Danchurchaid (Danish Church Aid) was distributed in Eritrea in April 1984 by the Evangelical Church of Eritrea (ECE), a sister church of the EECMY. The general secretary of the ECE described the distribution pattern: "The ECE has tried to reach all people in the region with the wheat. It distributes to all without regard to tribe or religion. Thus, Catholics, Moslems, and Orthodox share the gifts. Out of the 4,500 tons, only about 600 tons was given to members of the church. We have therefore gone to Akele Guzai area with 400 tons, an area where we have no congregation at all. The gift of wheat is given freely."[6]

Through its Department of Interchurch Aid and Development (DICAD), the Ethiopian Orthodox Church also became involved in early relief efforts in the northern provinces. A representative of DICAD participated in the three-person team, also including CRS and CRDA, that made the earliest survey trip into Tigray and Eritrea in September 1982 to assess the needs. During that year DICAD expended $135,326 in emergency aid and assisted 45,000 persons. It worked very closely with the RRC and through its major donors, World Vision International and the World Council of Churches.

Voluntary agencies from countries all over the world sent in money, commodities, and personnel. Much of this assistance was channeled through the CRDA, but by 1985, forty-six voluntary agencies were operating their own relief programs in Ethiopia. One of the earliest in the field was Save the Children (United Kingdom), which opened shelters and dispensed medical help at Korem in 1983–84.[7] World Vision contributed funds through the CRDA as early as 1982. Oxfam, an English agency, sent Dr. Paul Shears, a health consultant, in March 1983, and on the basis of his reports, began a fund-raising program in England and later sent in both food and personnel.[8] Both the International Committee of the Red Cross and the Ethiopian Red Cross were active in efforts to stem the tide of famine and starvation. As conditions worsened, it became increasingly clear that only the concerted aid of governments with access to massive supplies of grain could meet the crisis of hunger in Ethiopia.

Governmental Lethargy

Urgent appeals were directed to governments from many sources. In April 1983, the United Nations, speaking on behalf of the World Food Program (WFP), the World Health Organization (WHO), its Disaster Relief Office (UNDRO), and UNICEF, called on the governments of the world for relief assistance for one million people all across Ethiopia.[9] Voluntary agencies appealed to the governments in their home countries. International church networks urged their member churches to do likewise. In Europe appeals were made to the European Economic Community (EEC). Since 1974 Catholic Relief Services had had close ties with the U.S. government's Food for Peace program. Through this source CRS/Ethiopia now appealed for additional food on an emergency basis.

But as CRS discovered when it made its first application for a small emergency grant in December 1982, a combination of apathy and politics would bring about almost fatal delays in gaining access to these life-saving resources. Similar resistance was experienced by Oxfam in England, even after Dr. Paul Shears reported on his extensive tour of several famine-stricken provinces of Ethiopia. The reluctance of both the Thatcher government and the Reagan administration to offer aid was based on an unwillingness to bolster a Marxist government by feeding even its neediest citizens. Frustrated by the failure of the British government to respond, Oxfam finally purchased 10,000 tons of grain from private contributions and shipped it to Ethiopia at its own expense, hoping thereby to set an example for the British government.[10]

At the same time governments of the Scandinavian countries, Australia, and Canada, much more sensitive to the Ethiopian crisis and sympathetic to appeals from churches and voluntary agencies, responded promptly and generously with shipments of grain and other emergency commodities.

Since it was potentially the largest donor and actually was already operating a large, legally mandated program for emergencies in needy countries, the United States government opened itself to charges of neglecting starving people because of political animosity toward the Ethiopian government. Both the president of the United States and the administrator of AID (Agency for International Development) denied this charge vigorously, reminding their critics that the United States was by far the world's largest donor of food.

Nevertheless, as plans were being made in late 1982 for the new fiscal year beginning October 1, 1983, the administration removed all Ethiopia food programs from the congressional presentation of the budget. Since CRS depended on AID grants for its mother-child nutrition program, this action threatened serious contraction if not the termination of its regular seven-year-old nutrition program in Ethiopia, just at the time the real emergency was beginning.

Peggy Sheehan, coordinator of the AID Food for Peace Program, announced to CRS that the Development Coordination Committee, an interagency group in Washington that approved food allocations, had taken this action because the Ethiopian government was not putting enough of its own support into the program of hunger relief. Sheehan asked

CRS to request the Ethiopian government to allocate a million dollars for transporting U.S. grain, to provide nutritionists, nurses, and free warehousing throughout the country — requests that a government in the midst of civil war, with a heavy investment in military hardware, would almost certainly reject, thereby providing the U.S. government further rationale for discontinuing its food aid.[11]

Transmitting such a request to the Ethiopian government as a condition for continuing U.S. aid would have cast CRS in the role of spokesperson for the U.S. government's policies. Refusing to play such a role, CRS prepared a carefully worded response to be delivered to David A. Korn, U.S. chargé d'affaires in Addis Ababa. Signed by Geraldine Sicola, CRS assistant country representative, it stated that CRS felt it was neither "appropriate or necessary" for CRS, as a private voluntary agency, to approach the Ethiopian government to urge its support in carrying out a U.S. government Title II (Food for Peace) program. At the same time it advised Mr. Korn that CRS was regularly receiving alarming reports from several regions of the country describing the deteriorating health and nutrition of the child population. In view of these critical conditions, CRS declared its intention to update its proposed Operational Plan for 1983–84 and probably to request additional emergency support. A concluding comment thanked the U.S. government for the assistance channeled through CRS for the previous seven years and anticipated "continued collaboration in carrying out the humanitarian mandate of Public Law 480."[12]

Private and Public Pressures

During the ensuing weeks and months of 1983 and 1984, relations between CRS and the offices of AID were strained almost to the breaking point. While AID employed tactics to obstruct and delay, CRS found strong allies in Congress and the press. CRS executives testified frequently before congressional committees, and reporters such as Jay Ross and

David Ottaway of the *Washington Post* and Judith Miller of the *New York Times* kept the growing Ethiopian crisis before the public eye.

In spite of the U.S. government's negative stance toward Ethiopian relief, CRS submitted applications to continue its regular food allocation for Fiscal Year 1984, beginning October 1, 1983, and also requested an emergency allocation for 1983 to establish a feeding program in Makelle town in Tigray province, where malnutrition and disease were already taking a heavy toll. Father Thomas Fitzpatrick, recently appointed CRS Ethiopia country representative, drew up a modest proposal for 838 tons of food and submitted it through the U.S. embassy in Addis Ababa on December 7, 1982.[13] At the same time he also requested an emergency shipment of 500 tons from the European Economic Community.

From December 1982 until May 1983, while the famine tightened its grip on Ethiopia's northern provinces, AID shuffled the request from one Washington office to another. No action was taken. Instead, AID officials expressed uncertainty over CRS's alleged lack of experience in the Makelle area and questioned the qualifications of ECS, the local organization selected to distribute the food. Some doubts were even expressed concerning the actual need for the program. In late March 1983, after three months of investigation, the request was forwarded from the AID office for East African Affairs to the office of the assistant administrator for Africa for additional review.

On March 28, 1983, the *Times* of London reported a rumor that food donated by the EEC was being diverted to the Ethiopian army or to the Soviet Union in payment for arms. Although these allegations had already been proven false by an EEC investigation, AID cabled the U.S. embassy in Addis Ababa on April 13, requesting further details. The embassy, which had supported the CRS request in December, responded immediately, reaffirming that the EEC had found no evidence supporting the allegations and urging immediate approval of the CRS request.

During the first week in May 1983, the AID administrator in Washington learned that an NBC television crew had been granted Ethiopian visas to develop a story on the drought, and visa requests for reporters from three national newspapers were pending. Only this report and the announcement by the chargé d'affaires in the U.S. embassy in Addis Ababa on May 5 that a state of disaster existed in Ethiopia moved the Development Coordination Committee to approve the 838-ton emergency request on May 7, 1983 — five months after it was first submitted. At the same time an emergency grant of $25,000, initiated by the U.S. embassy in Addis Ababa to assist in establishing the program at Makelle, was also approved in Washington.[14]

The relationships between the Ethiopian and American governments at this time were at an extremely low ebb. Mengistu's Marxist affiliation was of course the basic point of estrangement. But the failure of the Ethiopian government to compensate American citizens for properties confiscated at the time of the Revolution in 1974 and its failure to repay U.S. government loans for the purchase of military hardware also placed Ethiopia under the Hickenlooper and Brooke Amendments to the Foreign Assistance Act of 1961 and made it ineligible to receive any long-term development aid from the United States.[15] Moreover, a member of the U.S. embassy staff had recently been arrested and beaten by Ethiopian police. In the ensuing weeks, however, it became increasingly evident that neither the Congress nor the people of the United States regarded these as compelling enough reasons to allow thousands of children to starve, especially when American granaries were bursting with surplus food.

On June 1, 1983, Michigan Congressman Howard Wolpe sent a letter to AID administrator Peter McPherson, signed by seventy-four of his colleagues, urging more sensitivity to the Ethiopian crisis.[16] Shortly thereafter, the Senate passed a similar resolution, and finally the *Washington Post* published a series of articles by Jay Ross, beginning June 26, graphically describing the conditions in Ethiopia and the failure of the United States to respond. "Despite urgent appeals for international assistance while there is still time to save thousands of lives," Ross wrote, "the United States, the world's largest source of surplus food, has virtually turned its back on the potential disaster."[17] After calling the articles to the attention of his colleagues, Senator Edward Kennedy inserted them in the *Congressional Record*.

CRS as Catalyst

Responding to anguished appeals from its field staff in Ethiopia, CRS submitted an additional emergency request to AID for 4,500 tons of food on July 5, with the endorsement of the U.S. embassy in Addis Ababa. It was approved in nine days. In August an AID team visited Ethiopia, followed by a delegation from the House of Representatives that visited remote areas in Gondar. They returned with urgent pleas to the State Department and to AID for increased food and transport assistance. Shortly thereafter AID announced that beginning October 1, 1983, 16,000 tons of food would be available. They also granted $800,000 to the United Nations Disaster Relief Organization (UNDRO) for inland transport and air delivery of food.[18]

In July 1983, the CRS board of directors appointed a recently retired career diplomat as its first lay executive director. Lawrence Pezzullo, former U.S. ambassador in Uruguay and Nicaragua, was fully conversant with the operations of the U.S. government, both at home and overseas. Shortly after his arrival in New York, he opened a Washington office and put Robert McCloskey, former U.S. ambassador to Greece, Cyprus, and the Netherlands, in charge. He then named two other foreign service alumni to key positions in the CRS structure.

Pezzullo assumed the leadership of CRS just as the Ethiopian crisis was deepening. It was clear to him that only massive amounts of food, supplied by the governments of the world, could meet those needs. Pezzullo took office on July 5, 1983, the day the 4,500-ton CRS emergency grant for

Ethiopia was endorsed by the U.S. embassy in Addis Ababa. His first question to James DeHarpporte, CRS deputy director for Africa, was, "What's going on in Ethiopia?" It was followed by a request for a full briefing and appropriate action to encourage the restoration of Ethiopia by the U.S. government to the regular list of eligible aid recipients.[19]

For the Africa staff of CRS, Pezzullo's response to the Ethiopian crisis was a welcome signal of support. Kenneth Hackett, senior regional director for Sub-Sahara Africa in New York, and Michael Wiest, sub-regional director in Nairobi, Kenya, both seasoned veterans in the CRS system, spoke of Pezzullo's response as "a new breath of fresh air."[20] Pezzullo's vigorous leadership increased the effectiveness of CRS appeals for U.S. government support and encouraged his staff to explore creative methods for dealing with the mounting food crisis in Ethiopia. Reflecting on the 1982–85 struggle with the AID bureaucracy, Hackett later recalled that those very frustrations had played a role in suggesting to him the value of joint action among private relief agencies, and had thus also contributed to the eventual formation of the Ethiopian partnership.

Encouraged by AID's announced intent to receive new proposals for Ethiopia, CRS submitted a request for 16,000 tons of food in early November 1983 to feed 55,000 families in Tigray and Eritrea for nine months. Basic attitudes at AID, however, had not changed. The Food for Peace office recommended granting only half the request, or 8,000 tons, and six more months elapsed before final clearance. The Working Group of the Development Coordination Committee, whose approval was required for all grants, first delayed action on grounds of an overburdened agenda. In December, the U.S. embassy in Addis Ababa received a report alleging that large amounts of CRS vegetable oil were being sold in local markets. An immediate audit by CRS revealed that none of the contract numbers on the cans corresponded to those on cans received from AID by CRS in Ethiopia. AID was still not satisfied. Two months later officials advised CRS that the 8,000-ton grant would be still further delayed because of conflicting reports concerning the amount of food actually available in Ethiopia.[21]

In January 1984, the World Food Program (WFP) announced that the supply of food was adequate to supply all needs through 1984. But in late March an UNDRO team reported that there was only enough food in the country to last two more months, or until May 1984. While starving people continued to crowd into camps in Tigray and Wollo, an AID team spent sixteen days conducting its own survey, finally concluding that drought and hunger actually did exist in the north and that there should be no further delaying of urgently needed drought assistance.

On May 18, 1984, the Working Group of Washington's Development Coordination Committee finally approved the 8,000-ton grant, and the OFDA (Office for Foreign Disaster Assistance) approved $924,885 for inland transportation.[22] A request for the remaining 8,000 tons was submitted on July 20, accompanied by an urgent letter from Kenneth Hackett, reminding AID that the original request and an operational plan had been submitted in November 1983, eight months earlier.[23] He attached a group of cables from staff members in Ethiopia stressing the gravity of the situation. Rhonda Sarnoff, regional nutritionist for CRS, described an alarming deterioration of the adult population in southern Shoa and Sidamo, an ominous foreshadowing of a real increase in the number of orphans.[24] Thomas Fitzpatrick reported several thousand Afar people at the Catholic mission in Kobo. They had fled from the Danakil plains after losing all their livestock. Many had walked a distance of forty miles. "Most are badly wasted mothers and children," he wrote, "who have no choice but to wait for food or death by starvation."[25] "The need to respond is now," Hackett warned, "before thousands are dead." Approval of the second 8,000-ton request followed within two weeks.

While awaiting AID's approval of the two 8,000-ton requests, Father Thomas Fitzpatrick had explored possible alternative sources for emergency food. Through negotiations with local representatives in Addis Ababa, he secured commitments of 2,050 tons from the Mennonite Central Committee and 3,200 tons from the Canadian International Development Agency. This food was available for use anywhere in Ethiopia.[26]

Pressure exerted on the administration in Washington by members of Congress and by private voluntary agencies also resulted in the restoration to the 1983–84 federal budget of the regular nonemergency food program for Ethiopia.

Late in September 1984, in the wake of an announced relaxation in U.S. administration policy toward the Ethiopian crisis, CRS submitted a request to AID for an additional 32,559 tons of emergency food. The request was approved on November 17, but processing and shipping schedules did not permit the arrival of the food in Ethiopia until early 1985.[27] Nevertheless, these accumulated tonnages committed to CRS by the U.S. government, supplemented by other shipments consigned to the Lutheran World Federation from European donors, constituted a combined resource for the launching of a cooperative Nutrition Intervention Program, even before plans for a consortium had been finalized.

"Washington's process of approving food requests is a deliberate and time-consuming one at best."

"The problems of receiving the food in Ethiopia and transporting it inland were monumental....In a territory larger than France and Spain, with a population of 42 million, Ethiopia has about 2,500 miles of paved roads, 5,500 miles of gravel roads, and 3,000 miles of hard dirt roads."

"Without the strategic airlifts and airdrops at the right times and in the right places, thousands of persons would not have survived."

IV

Lifelines of Mercy ──────────────

If A FEW CHILDREN ARE HUNGRY, the direct, uncomplicated human response is simply, "Feed them." But if a million children are starving and they are 10,000 miles away, there are generally more questions than answers. Where can you get such amounts of food? What kind of food? How can you transport it? How pay for it? How distribute it? How many will die before you can reach them?

Early in November 1984, shortly after the dramatic television reports on the Ethiopian famine, a man of some means and compassion called the New York offices of CRS and inquired, "How much does a ton of grain cost?" He was advised by Beth Griffin, the CRS communications director, that even if the government donated it, the cost of transporting a ton of grain from an Ethiopian port to points of distribution would be about $140. "Well," he said, "I want to get each of my friends to sign up to buy several tons of food."

Griffin replied, "I applaud your idea. I think your initiative is fine, but I think you're going to have a hard time when you try to buy grain in less than several thousand tons at a time, and you try to arrange for shipping, and you try to arrange for somebody to meet your shipment at the other end. But," she said, "you go ahead and try to get your friends to do it. Here's the number of the Kansas City com-

modities people from the government who deal with grain.
But keep my number, just in case."

About two months later the man called back and said,
"Ms. Griffin, you were right. The idea was a fine one, but
the logistics were outrageous. So instead, I'm going to have
a cocktail party at my grandmother's place in the East 70s,
and I'm going to ask all my friends each to contribute the
$140."

"We ended up," Griffin reported, "getting a healthy check
from this man. He started out with what seemed like a log-
ical idea, but without much understanding of the logistics of
famine relief."[1]

Food from America

The availability of U.S. food for international emergency relief dates from 1954. In that year Congress passed Public
Law 480, the Agricultural Trade Development & Assistance
Act, popularly known as "Food for Peace." Title II of the act
provides for donations of food "to meet famine or other urgent relief requirements, to combat malnutrition especially in
children, and to promote economic and community development."

When the Ethiopian crisis developed and emergency food
became essential, CRS was in an especially favorable position with respect to the food program of the U.S. government. Since 1975 it had been delivering PL-480 food around
the world — in Ethiopia and twenty other African countries,
in Asia, the Middle East, and Latin America. It was one
of the few agencies conducting mother-child feeding programs, aimed at improving the health of children under five
years of age and lactating mothers. At the time the Ethiopian
famine broke, CRS was handling 93 percent of all PL-480
food being shipped through voluntary agencies to Africa. Its
staff was familiar with the processes employed by the U.S.
government and the practices of African host governments.
Their operations were therefore highly regarded by officials

of Food for Peace, the office within the Agency for International Development that handled food aid.

Food for Peace ordinarily planned its total grants program and was assigned a budgetary appropriation based on a fiscal year beginning October 1 and ending September 30. Requests for aid submitted in April or May for the coming fiscal year were processed through the summer, usually requiring about six months lead time, for implementation in the fall. Emergency requests required special action and often a supplemental appropriation from Congress. This happened when political controversy delayed even CRS's small emergency requests for several months in 1982 and 1983.

Washington's process of approving food requests is a deliberate and time-consuming one at best. All food requests to AID must be accompanied by a detailed plan of operation, including a narrative description of how the commodities will be distributed once they arrive in the country, who the major actors are, and what kind of support system has been established. When these documents reach the Food for Peace office in Washington, they are referred to the Development Coordinating Committee, a rather loose-knit body with representatives from the Departments of State, Agriculture, and Commerce, the Office of Management and Budget, Food for Peace, and the National Security Council. Food for Peace, as a division within AID, becomes the advocate for the request. If the request is approved, CRS in New York is notified and that approval is communicated to the field. Such approval usually represents a twelve-month commitment by the government for food against the agency's operational plan.

On the basis of this commitment, the CRS field office normally issues a "call forward" of the commodities in quarterly allocations, in order to avoid overstocking the in-country warehouses and to assure a regular supply in the pipeline. Specific ports of arrival are designated for each shipment.

The "call forward" comes back to the CRS New York office, which enters it on an appropriate form and sends it to the U.S. Department of Agriculture. The department gath-

ers requests from all private voluntary agencies according to
the commodities requested — grain, milk powder, or edible
oils. If, for example, grain is involved, "an invitation to bid"
is dispatched to large milling companies, which then submit
bids on certain portions of the overall tonnage.

The Department of Agriculture then reviews the bids and
issues "public awards notices" to those who have offered
to sell at the lowest price. Steamship lines are notified that
these commodities are being purchased by the U.S. government from a particular miller for delivery to designated seaports in the U.S. at a particular time. The commodities arrive
at the seaport, properly bagged or packaged, numbered, and
marked as belonging to CRS.

Competing shipping companies then quote to the Department of Agriculture what their rates will be to pick up that
shipment and transport it to the overseas destination. A section of the Department of Agriculture located in Kansas City
digests all these shipping rates and determines the lowest.

It then becomes the responsibility of the CRS shipping
department to negotiate with the shippers, either to accept
the lowest bid or, if experience has demonstrated another
shipper to be especially dependable, to induce that shipper
to meet the lower competitive bid. These procedures, and the
additional requirement that 60 percent of the shipments must
travel on U.S. flaglines, are mandated by U.S. law governing food aid. Once the ship has left port, the CRS shipping
department must follow its course on a daily basis and be
ready to make adjustments in case of delays, storms, or ad-
verse conditions at the port of destination. In some cases,
the shipment must be diverted to another destination.

According to the agreements drawn up between the
CDAA/E partners in Ethiopia, CRS was designated as the
sole applicant for emergency food from the U.S. government
for distribution in Ethiopia. It was therefore responsible for
all logistical and financial arrangements for U.S. food, such
as port handling, shipping, inland transport to primary distribution points in Ethiopia, and ultimately also for reporting
and accounting.

For both the U.S. government and agencies like CRS, the suddenness and the size of the expansion of the Ethiopian program placed a heavy burden on logistic resources. Ordinary planning and budgetary procedures were strained. Food for Peace had to go back to Congress and ask for more money in the face of great political tension. Staff members of both public and private agencies found themselves working long hours to handle increased administrative and operational responsibilities.[2]

Food from Around the World

Procedures varied in other countries, where churches and agencies operating programs in Ethiopia either purchased food or requested it from their governments. The Italian government provided some food shipments directly to ECS, and Caritas/Germany served as the general sponsor agency for the Caritas network, channeling food and supplies from members, both through the partnership and directly to ECS.

In Australia, Canada, and the Scandinavian countries contributions were solicited from the governments by the service agencies and societies related to the Lutheran churches in those countries, such as Lutherhjaelpen in Sweden, Danchurchaid in Denmark, Canadian Lutheran World Relief in Canada, and Das Diakonische Werk or Brot für die Welt in the Federal Republic of Germany. In these cases the agencies arranged for ocean transport, usually asking for a government subsidy. As shipments arrived in Ethiopian ports, they were consigned to the Lutheran World Federation, which then handled port clearances and arranged transportation to primary distribution centers.

LWF also was the consignee for shipments authorized by the European Economic Community (EEC), an association of nations including the Federal Republic of Germany, France, Belgium, Netherlands, Denmark, the United Kingdom, Italy, and Ireland. Although most of the emergency assistance given by the EEC was allocated directly to recipient governments, requests from nongovernmental organizations (NGOs) were also considered.

According to procedures established by the EEC, qualified NGOs submitted their requests to an agency called Euronaid, a nonprofit association of nongovernmental organizations with offices in the Netherlands. Euronaid then transmitted the requests to a Food Aid Committee of the European Commission for evaluation. Grants were made within budgetary limits set by the EEC. Arrangements for the shipping of food were handled by CEBEMO, a Dutch organization that directed the transportation from European to Ethiopian ports. As consignee for the shipments, LWF received them, arranged for inland transport to primary distribution points, and was responsible for reporting on the arrival and proper use of the food.[3]

Once in Ethiopia: Roads, Trucks, and Mountains

If the logistic demands strained the procedures and personnel in donor countries in Europe and North America, the problems of receiving the food in Ethiopia and transporting it inland were monumental. Ethiopia had only two seaports, Massawa and Assab, and access to a third, in the neighboring country of Djibouti. Although probably better equipped than the ports of most other African countries, their facilities were not at first able to handle adequately the massive shipments of grain and supplies. Moreover, one of the ports, Massawa, was located in the part of the country in which a twenty-eight-year-old civil war was being fought.

At the outset, Assab, the most heavily used port, was able to clear 3,000 tons per day, partly because food arriving from the United States had already been bagged and was brought to the docks on LASH (Lighter Aboard Ship) barges. The mother ship, which carried up to eighty-five barges, each with a capacity of 370–75 tons, remained outside the harbor, put down the barges, and then continued on its way, avoiding a long wait for a berth. Ships not equipped with

these facilities often had to wait in a crowded harbor for
several days. Eventually, however, the U.S. government discouraged the use of the barges because many of them were
unseaworthy. Frequently, the loaded barges were allowed to
stand untended in the harbor while captains of conventional
cargo ships pressured port officials to unload their vessels.[4]

When the food shipments consigned to private relief
agencies first began to arrive in Ethiopia, the agencies were
able to share government warehousing facilities at the ports.
Since large shipments consigned to the Ethiopian government for its own relief program were also arriving, warehouse space was often crowded, making it necessary to stack
sacks of grain temporarily on the open docks. Even when
covered by heavy tarpaulins, these stacks were vulnerable to
infrequent but unpredictable rainstorms. The extent of damage was generally minor in relation to the huge amounts of
grain being moved, but such circumstances provided occasion for copy-hungry journalists to write about "food rotting
on the docks while thousands are starving in camps."

The task of moving shipments out of the ports was the
responsibility of the agency importing the food. For the ecumenical partners, this important process was directed by
Negash Garedew, an Ethiopian transportation specialist. Negash had served as the Ethiopian government's first manager
of ports, as deputy minister of transport, and, later, as a
consultant to one of Ethiopia's major shipping companies.
Under his supervision, shipping documents were processed
through customs and delivered to the Marine Transport Service, which was responsible for clearing the food shipments
from the port and loading them on trucks for inland transport.

Five primary inland distribution points were designated,
to which the arriving shipments were sent, usually by truck.
Food entering the port of Massawa was brought to Asmara. Shipments entering at Assab were forwarded to Addis
Ababa, Nazareth, and Dessie. Djibouti arrivals were sent to
Dire Dawa on the country's only railroad. The administration of each of these centers was placed under one of the

partner agencies, which was then responsible for supplying outlying distribution points in the area, according to carefully programmed allocations.[5]

In a territory larger than France and Spain, with a population of 42 million, Ethiopia has about 2,500 miles of paved roads, 5,500 miles of gravel roads, and 3,000 miles of hard dirt roads, and some of the most rugged terrain of any country in the world. Inland transport presents enormous problems. Paavo Faerm, LWF resident representative in Addis Ababa, described a mountainous area in northern Shoa. No means of communication existed other than footpaths. At one time the relief operation there mobilized 3,000 donkeys and mules to transport food to the people. It was "food-for-work," said Faerm, for the donkeys and mules as well as for the people, because part of the food had to be given to the animals to keep them moving up and down the steep footpaths.[6] When asked what was the greatest need of the agencies at work in Ethiopia, with the exception of food to feed the starving, one veteran field staffer replied, "Trucks, trucks, and more trucks!"

Some of the trucks belonging to the government-operated National Transport Corporation (NATRACO) and to the Ketena System, a large fleet of commercial vehicles coordinated by the government, were also available to the voluntary agencies upon payment of standard usage fees. Most of the food transported by voluntary agencies was carried in NATRACO or Ketena trucks. Army trucks, whose first responsibility was to move military supplies and troops within the battle zones in Eritrea and Tigray, provided erratic supplements.[7]

Even before the organization of the partnership, each private agency operated a few of its own trucks. The CRDA had established a fleet that was available to its members on request. In March 1984, LWR, CRS, and CWS — members of the consortium Interchurch Response for the Horn of Africa — secured funds from AID to purchase five trucks for the CRDA fleet. As the number of their trucks grew, the private agencies had to engage full-time mechanics to service and repair their fleets. Both LWF and CRS established complete maintenance and repair shops to accommodate their own trucks and those of several other voluntary agencies. EECMY/LWF operated thirty-nine trucks, ECS forty-two, and CRS twenty-four. In October 1985, CRS completed negotiations with a firm in Kenya called Contrax to lease an entire additional fleet of fifty-five trucks, which, together with those of other partners, were also used for transport of food and supplies.[8]

For the long haul from seaport to primary distribution centers twenty-two-ton tractor-trailer trucks were the chief carriers. German Mercedes and Italian Fiats were the most dependable models, and for these, as well as for all others, spare parts were as important as the trucks themselves. For shorter distances and more rugged travel, five-ton and seven-and-a-half-ton trucks with four-wheel drive were used.

Elaborate procedural handbooks to guide truckers and warehouse personnel, prepared by the Logistics Department of CRS, were written by Robert Roche, Negash Garedew, and Cameron Peters. The care with which warehouse personnel and truck drivers were instructed and meticulous record-keeping on each truckload from departure point to destination kept losses through damage or theft to a minimum. Considering the primitive condition of many of the more remote roads and the constant hazards of military action in the northern provinces, it was remarkable that only a few trucks were lost.[9]

Airlifts and Airdrops

Although trucks were the only practicable means of transporting the thousands of tons of relief food throughout Ethiopia, there were times and places where the use of air transport became crucial. Travel into the country from abroad was virtually exclusively by air. Although major airlines such as Alitalia, Lufthansa, and British Airways flew regularly into Addis Ababa, the well-equipped fleet of 757s operated by the Ethiopian Airlines, probably Africa's best, provided the most dependable and frequent air service.

Most travel by the staffs of voluntary agencies was by motor vehicle. Every agency maintained its own fleet of passenger vehicles for transportation within Addis Ababa and four-wheel drive vehicles for travel into rural areas. But in a country with such rugged terrain and so few roads, light planes were the most efficient means of personal travel, and many towns of moderate size maintained airstrips. Visitors on limited time schedules were often booked on regular inland flights of Ethiopian Airlines or on planes made available by the Ethiopian government. The RRC had its own DC-9. A few voluntary agencies, such as World Vision and the French medical organization, Médecins sans Frontières, operated their own small aircraft. Because of the need to accommodate the Soviet-subsidized Ethiopian Air Force, several airports were able to handle large cargo planes such as C-130s.

In the wake of the BBC and NBC television broadcasts of October 23–24, 1984, both governments and private relief agencies sent emergency aid of all kinds into Ethiopia by air. International mercy flights from countries in all parts of the world brought clothing, blankets, tents, and medicines to supply hundreds of camps where food was distributed. Among the first to respond were Caritas/Germany, Lutheran World Federation, and Catholic Relief Services, which gathered funds, arranged a charter, and landed their first planeload of food in Makelle on November 2, little more than a week after the TV broadcasts. The Ethiopian Catholic Secretariat in Asmara coordinated the receiving end of this air mission.[10]

When Commissioner Dawit Wolde Giorgis of the RRC returned to Ethiopia in early November 1984, from a mission to Europe, England, and North America to plead for more aid, he described Addis Ababa's Bole Airport as "full of foreign planes — the RAF, the German Air Force, Soviet planes, and many chartered planes shuttling relief items from Europe and the Middle East."[11]

In some of the more remote locations where roads were poor and landing strips nonexistent, airdrops were used to supply emergency needs. One such drop in Wollo province was described by an observer who watched the operation from a Polish helicopter. The drop was carried out by a pilot and crew from the British Air Force, flying an American-made C-130 Hercules transport plane.

Each 100-pound sack of grain was enclosed in another, larger loose sack. If the inner sack broke, the grain would be held safely in the second enclosing bag. A load of one hundred such bags, covered by heavy plastic sheeting, was bound by ropes to a wooden pallet mounted on rails and fitted with small steel rollers so it could be easily pushed out of the plane.

The drop zone was marked by a big blue arrow on the ground. The pilot made three successive passes over the drop zone at treetop level to unload his 15-ton cargo. At the designated moment the cargo master kicked the load out of the back end of the plane. When the pallet hit the ground, it broke and sent the sacks of grain rolling along the ground like marbles. Between each of the three runs of the C-130, a ground crew rushed out to the drop site and carried off the sacks. After completing its three runs, the C-130 flew back to Addis Ababa, reloaded, and returned to repeat the operation. Four such airdrops were accomplished in a single day. On the occasion described by this observer, 60 tons of grain were dropped. Only one sack was broken.[12]

Compared with the hundreds of thousands of tons moved by truck along Ethiopia's limited road system, the volume of food that had to be transported by air within Ethiopia was not large. Nevertheless, without the strategic airlifts and airdrops at the right times and in the right places, thousands of persons in otherwise inaccessible locations would not have survived.

"In one of the most successful recent instances of ecumenical cooperation, three American-based agencies — Church World Service, Catholic Relief Services, and Lutheran World Relief — joined together in 1980 in the Interchurch Response for the Horn of Africa (ICRHA)."

"The fourteen representatives of the proposed partners who gathered in Geneva approved a joint appeal to raise $100 million (for African relief)....The total response from churches, private agencies, and governments for Ethiopian relief would eclipse the $100 million goal established by the CDAA for the whole of Africa."

"Persistent pressure on Congress by CRS, LWR, CWS, and others to secure emergency food grants from the U.S. government for Ethiopia finally began to bear fruit."

"Before the end of October an airlift initiated by Caritas/Germany and supported by CDAA members in Europe flew 3,000 tons of food from Asmara and Assab to the beleaguered inland cities of Makelle and Korem."

V

The Ecumenical Impulse ———

WHEN DR. EUGENE RIES, executive director of the Lutheran World Federation's Department of World Service, extended an invitation on February 1, 1984, to representatives of the World Council of Churches, Catholic Relief Services, and Caritas Internationalis to join together in seeking relief for the drought-stricken continent of Africa, he was in one sense asking them to relive a chapter of their own history.[1] Each of these international church agencies had begun its work of compassion in response to the needs of the war-ravaged continent of Europe following World War II.

Each of them had for many years been involved in Africa, either as individual agencies or through their constituent members. They had also been associated cooperatively in individual African countries through agencies such as the Christian Relief and Development Association in Ethiopia, established after the famine of 1972–74 to provide information and coordinate the assistance programs of its members. During the Biafra War in Nigeria in 1968–70, Protestant and Catholic agencies had formed a consortium called Joint Church Action that operated an airlift to feed Biafrans victimized by the starvation tactics of the Nigerian government and its British allies.

In one of the most successful recent instances of ecumenical cooperation, three American-based agencies — Church
World Service, Catholic Relief Services, and Lutheran World
Relief — joined together in 1980 in the Interchurch Response
for the Horn of Africa (ICRHA). Through the ICRHA, these
partners rehabilitated hospital facilities for Ethiopian refugees
in Somalia and provided health care, water, and agricultural
programs that encouraged self-reliance among the beneficiaries. Of special significance for the future were the close
personal and institutional relations that developed among
the leaders of the three cooperating agencies: Norman Barth
of Lutheran World Relief, Richard Butler of Church World
Service, and Lawrence Pezzullo of Catholic Relief Services.
The creation of this mutual trust was an important factor
in establishing both the CDAA in Europe and the CDAA in
Ethiopia. The ICRHA itself became involved in the famine
relief programs in Ethiopia in 1984, when it secured a grant
of $500,000 from the U.S. Office for Foreign Disaster Assis-
tance (OFDA) for the purchase of a small fleet of Mercedes
trucks for CRDA.[2]

A Consortium for All Africa

Those who assembled in Geneva on February 15, 1984,
in response to Dr. Ries's invitation were initiating the first
international Protestant–Roman Catholic venture undertaken
on behalf of an entire continent. The impulse for Ries's
letter had come from the Emergencies Working Group of
Lutheran World Service at a meeting in Bossey, Switzerland, in November 1983. Ludwig Geissel, a German lay
leader whose experience in relief and rehabilitation work
extended back to the European recovery programs following World War II, had presented an outline for a joint
Protestant-Catholic response to the plight of 150 million
people in Africa suffering from the effects of widespread
drought. Geissel stated his conviction that while immediate
relief was important, longer-range aid for all of Africa was

equally important. He therefore proposed that LWF, WCC, CI, and CRS join in an appeal to raise $100 million for both African relief and development. The accent, he felt, should be upon those drought-affected countries in which the international partners already had counterpart churches or related agencies. Beyond raising $100 million, the appeal should seek to arouse and inform public opinion and stimulate action by governments and international agencies for expanded programs of relief and economic and social development.[3]

The fourteen representatives of the proposed partners who gathered in Geneva approved a joint appeal to raise $100 million. Their decision was made public at a press conference one month later, on March 15. The official release emphasized that while the appeal itself would be coordinated through the international agencies, the programs of relief and development would be carried out in African countries by local churches and societies.[4] To emphasize this focus, Emmanuel Abraham, president of the Ethiopian Evangelical Church Mekane Yesus, was invited to make the formal presentation at the press conference. "Many African countries have been suffering for fifteen years from drought," he declared. "The call for common action in this emergency situation from the Catholic and Protestant agencies is becoming ever stronger. Almost every third African is or soon will be suffering from hunger."[5]

At the meeting on March 15, a coordinating committee of six Catholics and six Protestants was established. Ludwig Geissel was asked to serve as chairman, and Brian Neldner, an Australian who directed the relief and development program for Lutheran World Service, as coordinating secretary. Gerhard Meier, executive director of Caritas Internationalis, the worldwide network of Catholic relief agencies, became deputy chairman. Representatives of the constituting partners and their related agencies in Europe and North America completed the twelve-person coordinating committee, divided equally between Protestants and Catholics.[6]

To establish a common context for the anticipated appeal, members agreed to conduct an inventory of their current aid programs in Africa, to project new ventures for the next one to two years, and to report at the next meeting on April 17 in Geneva. The new commitments were to be over and above the aggregate $270 million total already designated by the agencies for their current programs throughout Africa. The name of the new association would be Churches Drought Action in Africa (CDAA).[7]

At a June meeting in Rome, Brian Neldner reported that the cooperating agencies had already given assurances for $100 million, the full amount of the appeal: $54 million in cash and 112,413 tons of food valued at $500 per ton, or $56 million. In addition, the Lutheran World Federation and Caritas Internationalis had each committed $100,000 for a comprehensive study on the root causes of hunger in Africa, to be led by Dr. Sibusisu Bengu, a South African on the staff of the Lutheran World Federation.[8]

Worsening Crisis in Ethiopia

By the time of the next meeting of CDAA in late October, the world's attention had been riveted on a single African country, Ethiopia, already in the midst of the century's worst famine. The total response from churches, private agencies, and governments for Ethiopian relief would eclipse the $100 million goal established by the CDAA for the whole of Africa.

CDAA partners had agreed that the aid programs supported through their appeal would supplement ongoing efforts throughout Africa, but especially in the twenty-four countries identified by the United Nations Economic Commission for Africa as most seriously affected by drought. Since members of CDAA were already supporting relief and development projects in many of them, each agency was expected simply to accelerate its fund-raising efforts and initiate new approaches to private donors and to governments.

The special message of CDAA was that the continent of Africa as a whole was in serious trouble. Nations and people in the northern hemisphere needed to understand this clearly before time ran out.

At the initial invitational meeting of CDAA, LWF's Eugene Ries identified seven countries, including Ethiopia, in which Lutheran World Service was already cooperating with church, governmental, and intergovernmental partners. Without specifically mentioning Ethiopia, Kenneth Hackett, CRS senior regional director for Sub-Sahara Africa, made reference at the same meeting to the increased pressure being exerted on the U.S. government, which, he said, had already enabled agencies such as CRS to expand their assistance considerably.[9] The lobbying effort in the United States was especially focused on Ethiopian assistance, inasmuch as strained political relations had placed all U.S. aid to Ethiopia in jeopardy. In conversations following the February 15 meeting, Hackett had discussed with Robert Quinlan, CRS representative in Geneva, the possibility of cooperation in Ethiopia at a national level, modeled after the Interchurch Response of Protestants and Catholics in Somalia, and the possible use of existing cooperative agencies such as the CRDA in Ethiopia. Either of these, he suggested, could be carried out as an expression of the broad mandate of CDAA.[10]

During the weeks following the March 15 meeting of CDAA, while member agencies were soliciting new commitments against the $100 million goal, persistent pressure on Congress by CRS, LWR, CWS, and others to secure emergency food grants from the U.S. government for Ethiopia finally began to bear fruit. Between May and August 1984 CRS requests for 16,000 tons of food, valued at $8 million, and almost $1 million for inland transport, were approved by AID. Although these grants and the prospects for further increases were not the direct results of the CDAA appeal, they coincided with both the objectives and the timing of the $100 million CDAA appeal on behalf of victims of the African famine.

More importantly, these grants enabled CRS to step up its emergency programs in areas such as Makelle and Kobo, where CRS had distributed its first emergency grants from AID, beginning in May 1983. They also opened the way for closer on-site cooperation with the Lutherans.

On July 20, 1984, Geraldine Sicola, CRS assistant country representative in Addis Ababa, cabled Kenneth Hackett in New York that the Mekane Yesus Church, which had also been distributing food in Wollo province since April 1983, was interested in joining with CRS in a nutrition intervention program. EECMY/LWF had recently received a shipment of 5,000 tons of wheat from the Swedish National Committee of LWF, to be distributed in Wollo and Kambatta/Hadya, and had expressed a willingness to lend CRS 900 tons of grain until the next CRS emergency shipment arrived in September.[11]

Rhonda Sarnoff, regional nutritionist for CRS, reported to Hackett that several NGOs in southern Shoa and Sidamo had requested additional emergency assistance for their programs, but because of shortages, CRS had been unable to respond. Its own program in those areas was being maintained only because EECMY/LWF had been able to provide grain from its sources to feed 10,000 families. If an adequate supply of cereal and oil were available, she wrote, twice the number of families currently receiving rations could be reached.[12]

In both cases where Mekane Yesus had agreed to supply food to CRS, it also agreed to work cooperatively with CRS and to carry out its program according to the nutrition intervention guidelines adopted by CRS.[13] On September 6, 1984, Dr. Solomon Gidada, development director of the Mekane Yesus Church, signed an official agreement with CRS, embracing those guidelines. "It has been realized," wrote Leo Siliamaa, deputy resident representative for LWF in Addis Ababa, "that only through concerted and coordinated efforts can the situation be improved."[14]

Ethiopian Government Celebrates while People Starve

In spite of the deteriorating conditions in many parts of the country, the Ethiopian government had not yet officially acknowledged that famine conditions existed. In March 1984, its own Relief and Rehabilitation Commission had estimated the food shortage in the country at 950,000 tons, but requested only 450,000 tons from world sources. Commissioner Dawit admitted that the request was scaled down because the Ethiopian government believed donors would doubt the capacity of Ethiopian facilities to handle the larger amount.[15] In any event, the action had the practical effect of writing off 50 percent of the five million persons in Ethiopia affected by the drought and famine.

In preparation for the tenth anniversary of the Revolution on September 12, 1984, the city of Addis Ababa had been treated to an expensive facelift. Streets were paved; public buildings were repainted. A 20-ton bronze statue of Lenin, gift of the Soviet Union, was installed alongside the former emperor's Jubilee Palace. North Korean and East German experts instructed the populace in parade and marching techniques and decorated Addis Ababa's Revolution Square with monumental portraits of Marx, Engels, and Lenin. Estimates of the expenditures for the lavish celebration ranged from $150 to $200 million. In a six-hour address glorifying the achievements of the Revolution, Lt. Col. Mengistu Haile Mariam made no mention of the specter of starvation already stalking the villages and farms in half his country's provinces.[16]

For several weeks before the celebration, travel within the country was sharply restricted. Reporters and photographers were refused permits to visit the northern provinces. Among the reporters barred from the famine areas during the festivities in Addis Ababa were David Ottaway of the *Washington Post* and Judith Miller of the *New York Times.* Both filed stories based on personal interviews with relief workers who had first-hand knowledge of the starvation that was taking a grim toll in the north while the capital city

celebrated. Ottaway cited several reports from foreign relief workers that "the government has been trying to hold
off the rush of starving peasants into the bigger towns and
cities, particularly the capital, Addis Ababa, to the point
of stopping them on the road and sending them back by
truck."[17]

These stories, which appeared simultaneously on September 18, gave renewed impetus to the efforts of advocates
of increased emergency aid. Congressman Mickey Leland
of Texas ordered the articles inserted into the *Congressional
Record*.[18] On September 19, at a meeting of all private voluntary agencies in Washington, Peter McPherson, administrator
of AID, announced a change in U.S. government policy toward food aid for Ethiopia. Declaring that "a hungry child
knows no politics," McPherson said it was the intention of
the U.S. government to shoulder a major part of the world's
food aid to Ethiopia, using private agencies as channels for
distribution.[19]

Putting Together a Partnership

On September 26, the CRDA sent out a message to potential
donors all over the world, signed by its twenty-six member
agencies, describing the catastrophic conditions. "Ethiopia,"
it declared, "has not experienced a food shortage of this
magnitude within living memory. In terms of geographical
extent and population affected, it vastly exceeds in severity the drought and famine of 1973, when three regions
(provinces) were affected. Today 12 of the 14 regions are
affected by drought. Death by starvation is occurring in six
of these. More than a million people are estimated to be affected by food shortage."[20]

Lawrence Pezzullo, CRS executive director, telephoned
Kenneth Hackett, his Africa director, who was on a field trip
in Lesotho in southern Africa. "The press is hitting hard in
Ethiopia," he told Hackett. "You better go right up there and
find out what's going on, so we can respond."[21]

Hackett left immediately for Nairobi to confer with CRS sub-regional director Michael Wiest. After waiting a few days for entry visas, both men flew from Nairobi to Addis Ababa, arriving on the weekend of September 29–30. Over Sunday dinner at the Ghion Hotel in Addis Ababa, Hackett and Wiest heard firsthand corroboration of the CRDA report from Geraldine Sicola, Susan Barber, CRS drought relief coordinator, and Brother Cesare Bullo, who brought eye-witness accounts from Makelle in the province of Tigray. On Monday, October 1, Hackett cabled New York that the famine was "the biggest thing we have ever seen," and he and Wiest sat down in the CRS offices to brainstorm how best to meet the crisis.[22]

It had already become apparent to Susan Barber and Geraldine Sicola that the task was far too large for any single agency to handle. Neither the few thousand tons of emergency food CRS had received from the U.S. nor the food and supplies other agencies had brought in from Europe, Australia, and Canada could begin to meet the needs of the thousands of people Brother Bullo had seen struggling into the camps of his home city of Makelle, much less the six million people throughout the country estimated to be endangered by the drought.

Recalling other instances of interagency cooperation in Biafra, Zimbabwe, and Somalia, Hackett and Wiest considered the possibilities of a coalition for Ethiopia. After spending much of Monday outlining a plan, they plotted out a week-long round of meetings, beginning with the Catholic cardinal, Archbishop Paulos, and the executive of the Ethiopian Catholic Secretariat, Father Stephanos Tedla. Hackett and Wiest called successively on colleagues of the Lutheran World Federation and the Mekane Yesus Church, World Vision International, and the CRDA. From each agency they received positive responses.

After briefing CRS in New York by phone concerning a possible cooperative effort and the positive response of other private agencies, Hackett and Wiest moved on to the public agencies. They met with Dawit Wolde Giorgis, Commissioner of the RRC; Trevor Paige of the World Food Program; David Korn, U.S. chargé d'affaires; Ronald Ulrich and Richard Gold of USAID.

By Thursday, October 4, they had progressed far enough to stage a planning meeting with potential partners. Dr. Solomon Gidada of the Mekane Yesus Church, Niels Nikolaisen of the Lutheran World Federation, Brother Augustine O'Keefe of CRDA, Father Thomas Fitzpatrick of CRS, and Father Stephanos Tedla of the ECS joined them around a table at the Catholic Secretariat. Together they sketched out on a map areas of the country that each partner might serve most effectively. CRDA would be responsible for Sidamo and Gamo Gofa; ECS for Eritrea and Tigray; EECMY/LWF for Wollo and Shoa; and World Vision for Bale, Hararge, and Gondar.

They also agreed that CRS should approach the United States government for at least 150,000 to 200,000 tons of emergency food. In view of its long experience with the U.S. government program, Hackett suggested that CRS coordinate and handle the logistics of the operation. The other partners, with local networks and personnel already in place, would handle the distribution. Joint Church Action for Famine Relief (JCAFR) would be the name of the consortium.

Within the week, virtually every base had been touched. Meetings with Tony Atkins and Ross Kerr of World Vision International and with Archbishop Thomas White, papal pro-nuncio for Ethiopia, rounded out the schedule. Hackett and Wiest spent Sunday at the CRS office, writing up the plans that had been developed during the week. They even found time to contact Robert Quinlan, director of the Geneva office of CRS, to ask his help in inviting Peter Lumb, recently retired from the CRS staff in Geneva, to come to Addis Ababa to work with the consortium in fine-tuning the structure and operational plan.[23]

An Appeal to the World

The next few days were fully as eventful as the week just ended. On Monday morning, October 8, the Ethiopian Relief and Rehabilitation Commission called a special donors' meeting at the Ghion Hotel to make a formal announcement that a famine emergency did exist. The meeting was attended by resident ambassadors, U.N. staff, and representatives of voluntary agencies. Commissioner Dawit alternately thanked the agencies for their help and scolded the governments for their apathy, singling out for special mention the United States, which, he said, "appears to have bowed out of its customary role of providing relief because of Ethiopia's close ties to the Soviet Union." This was too much for David Korn, chargé d'affaires at the U.S. embassy, who walked out of the meeting in protest.[24]

Following the RRC meeting at the Ghion Hotel, the Italian ambassador invited several of his diplomatic colleagues to his residence to discuss the commissioner's address. Archbishop Thomas White invited Kenneth Hackett and Michael Wiest to accompany him. As this distinguished group of diplomats and other visitors sat around the elegantly carved table in the embassy library, engaging in general conversation concerning the morning's presentation and remarking on reports that some donated cans of vegetable oil had appeared for sale in local markets, Michael Wiest interrupted the conversation. Courteously, but in a voice straining with emotion, he reminded the group that while they sat and talked, thousands of people in the camps were dying of starvation and disease. He described the experiences of Brother Cesare Bullo, director of a technical school for boys in Makelle, who had shared his personal experiences during the past week. One of the heroes in the battle against starvation, Brother Bullo had been obliged to assign young students from his school to bury the dead. Survivors were eating grass in their attempt to stay alive. Documented deaths were occurring at Makelle at the rate of fifteen to twenty-five per day. "And while all this is going on," Wiest said, "we keep talking and talking and talking about a can of food here and a can of food there. And nothing is happening." As he concluded his comments, his voice broke and he wept.

One of the persons present later observed, "The whole meeting changed. No one had anything more to say about the few cans of oil showing up in the market." Later on, this event was described as a "turning point" in the effort to secure food from European sources, as these ambassadors reported to their governments on the plight of Ethiopia.[25]

One reason things were so bad in and around Makelle was that even military-escorted trucks could not get through on a regular basis to Makelle, in Tigray province, from Asmara, the Eritrean capital. The 200-mile stretch of highway between these two cities, nominally under the control of Ethiopian government forces, was impassable because of guerrilla-style attacks by insurgent troops in both Eritrea and Tigray. From mid-August to mid-October 1984, no trucks at all reached Makelle. The destitute population in Makelle rose to 32,000. By October 15, food stocks on hand for all relief programs, including those of the ICRC, RRC, and CRS, were close to exhaustion. Virtually nothing was available for purchase in the local markets.

In spite of the high cost, the agencies on the spot, particularly ECS and CRS, turned to air transport. Urgent cables went out to New York and to Caritas Internationalis in Rome.[26] They responded. Before the end of October an airlift initiated by Caritas/Germany and supported by CDAA members in Europe at a cost of $1.2 million flew 3,000 tons of food from Asmara and Assab to the beleaguered inland cities of Makelle and Korem.

In announcing the airlift the CDAA Coordinating Committee also appealed to the Ethiopian government and the insurgent forces in Eritrea and Tigray "to stop the military activities and give free passage so that international aid organizations can provide massive emergency assistance to the starving people in the area."[27] Father Stephanos Tedla, director of the Ethiopian Catholic Secretariat, assumed responsibility for handling the arrival of the air cargoes through the ECS office in Asmara. The first flights of the chartered Transamerica planes landed in Makelle on November 2.

On October 10 Hackett and Wiest flew to Makelle and Kobo to observe for themselves the extent of the human disaster. The day following they parted company at Bole Airport in Addis Ababa. Wiest remained in Addis to begin the actual formation of a workable consortium. Hackett went on his way to Geneva, stopping briefly in Rome to brief the Vatican and officials of Caritas Internationalis. In Geneva he caught up with Lawrence Pezzullo, who had just completed an inspection of the earthquake disaster areas in southern Italy.

With Pezzullo when Hackett arrived on October 12 were Robert Quinlan of the Geneva office of CRS, Monsignor Robert Coll of the Rome office, and Father Robert Charlebois, senior CRS director for Eurasia, who were discussing with Pezzullo the possible merging of the CRS offices in Geneva and Rome.

After describing the critical famine situation in Ethiopia and the fast-moving events of the previous week, Hackett presented the plan he and Wiest proposed for a consortium. "We want to do what we've never done before," he told Pezzullo. "We've got partners who are ready to work with us." Given the overwhelming need and the indigenous resources available for distributing food, Hackett continued, "100,000 tons is just the beginning. It could go much further." Pezzullo thought about it, and said, "Yes. We have to do it!"

There was little time for consultation. It would obviously be necessary to secure official concurrence from the Lutheran World Federation and assurance of support from the Caritas network, but if CRS were to act in a coordinating role, someone would have to be appointed immediately to handle those responsibilities. Pezzullo telephoned New York to confer with his colleague Ambassador Robert McCloskey. Then he turned to Monsignor Coll and asked, "How about you, Bob?"[28]

Monsignor Coll had been assistant executive director of CRS in New York. Though he had never served in Africa, he was known to be a strong friend of CRS programs in Africa and a person of great energy and enthusiasm. Before Pezzullo returned to New York the following day, Coll agreed to go to Addis Ababa as the CRS representative. The responsibilities he would carry for CRS were not spelled out, nor was his intended role in the proposed consortium. Those who knew Monsignor Coll, however, must have known that it would be a leading role.

Drawing the Lines

On Sunday afternoon, October 14, Kenneth Hackett and Robert Quinlan met Brian Neldner, associate director of LWF's Department of World Service, at his home to discuss LWF participation in the proposed consortium.[29] Niels Nikolaisen, LWF resident representative in Ethiopia, had already given his approval. Neldner greeted the Ethiopian plan as a welcome outgrowth of the ecumenical spirit expressed in the CDAA, in which both LWF and CRS were participants. He did, however, anticipate some problems if the consortium should include World Vision International in its membership. Objecting primarily to its aggressive evangelistic and fund-raising techniques, two Scandinavian countries whose national churches were members of LWF had asked World Vision to discontinue operations in their parishes. During Hackett's brief visit in Rome some misgivings had also been expressed by Father Fauré of Cor Unum and by Cardinal Paulos and Father Stephanos in Addis Ababa. But for Hackett and Wiest the importance of maximizing the impact of food requests to the U.S. government and of establishing as comprehensive a distribution network as possible were overriding concerns.[30] A final decision on the inclusion of World Vision would rest with the Coordinating Committee of CDAA, scheduled to meet in Geneva on October 29.

Meanwhile, Peter Lumb had accepted the invitation from the consortium in Addis Ababa to serve as a temporary consultant in drawing up basic documents for the Joint Church

Action for Famine Relief (JCAFR). However, there had been no opportunity for him to confer in Geneva with either Hackett or Coll before he left for Ethiopia on October 15.

After securing an entry visa in Nairobi, Lumb flew to Addis Ababa, arriving on the morning of October 17. When he met the same afternoon with the entire group of potential partners, including World Vision and CRDA, it was immediately clear that there were differences to be worked out, both on basic principles and on the structure and operation of the consortium.[31] Tony Atkins of World Vision wanted further discussion of the geographic areas of responsibility. He also objected to CRS's limiting itself to a coordinating role, rather than becoming directly involved in the distribution of food like all other partners. The next meeting was set for October 22, when the group would begin preparation of guidelines for the cooperative program.

Discussions continued along the same line at this meeting, except that Atkins now urged setting a target of at least 300,000 tons of food instead of a more modest goal of 150–200,000 tons. "World Vision," he said, "wants to shoot for the stars." Niels Nikolaisen warned against asking for more than the consortium could reasonably handle. The matter was left undecided.

The group, however, accepted the CRS proposal dividing the country among ECS, EECMY/LWF, World Vision, and CRDA. CRS was also approved as the coordinating agency in dealing with the U.S. government on behalf of the consortium. LWF undertook similar responsibility for requesting food from the European Economic Community.

At the conclusion of the meeting, Peter Lumb suggested four areas of discussion that should be addressed by small working groups: nutrition and food requirements, with Susan Barber of CRS as coordinator; logistics, Richard Venegoni, World Vision; administration, Augustine O'Keefe, CRDA; finances and budget estimates, Admasu Simeso, EECMY/LWF.[32]

Before the next general meeting of the consortium took place in Addis Ababa on October 29, developments in Eu-

rope had begun to cast doubt on the inclusion of World
Vision in the consortium. After the conversations at Brian
Neldner's home in Geneva on October 14, additional ob-
jections had been voiced by both Protestants and Catholics.
A meeting of the Emergency Committee of Caritas Internationalis in Rome on October 16 indicated its reservations.
Robert Quinlan, CRS representative in Geneva, known and
respected for his sensitivity to the ecumenical climate in
Geneva, advised his colleagues that the inclusion of World
Vision in the consortium would in all likelihood rule out the
support of the CDAA. Ludwig Geissel, chairman of its Coordinating Committee, Hans-Otto Hahn, director of Brot für
die Welt, and George Tsetsis, deputy director of the Commission on Inter-Church Aid, Refugee and World Service of
the World Council of Churches, were adamantly opposed.

By October 23 the position of CDAA members in Geneva
was clear. Hackett notified Lawrence Pezzullo in New York
and Michael Wiest in Addis Ababa. Wiest conveyed the message to Father Stephanos Tedla of ECS, to Dr. Solomon
of EECMY, and to Niels Nikolaisen of LWF. Pezzullo in
turn notified Dr. Thomas Houston, president of World Vision
International, that membership in the consortium would be
limited to agencies related to CDAA in Geneva.[33]

On October 24, the day Mohammed Amin's films were
broadcast nationally by NBC-TV in New York, Pezzullo appointed two CRS task forces to deal with the Ethiopia emergency. He headed the U.S. group himself, supported by
Robert McCloskey, CRS officer in Washington, handling resources and publicity, and Kenneth Hackett in New York,
handling operations. To lead the task force in Ethiopia, he
named Monsignor Robert Coll, with Peter Lumb handling
design and Susan Barber drought coordination. In a cable accompanying his announcement to all CRS programs,
Pezzullo stated that CRS would work closely with ECS,
EECMY/LWF, and CRDA as distributors of U.S. food. As
agreed by the partner agencies in Addis Ababa, CRS would
take the role of coordinator to insure effective use of resources and minimize duplication of efforts.[34]

The next day, Kenneth Hackett, who had just arrived in New York from Geneva, sent telexes to Father Stephanos Tedla, Michael Wiest, and Brother Augustine O'Keefe in Addis Ababa, and to Robert Quinlan and Brian Neldner in Geneva, incorporating a proposed letter of agreement in accordance with the field design described by Pezzullo. "The media blitz that has started in the United States," he cabled Neldner, "impels us to make some rather immediate decisions on our cooperation." He requested an immediate response to strengthen his hand for a scheduled meeting with AID in Washington, at which he intended to make a request for 200,000 tons of emergency food on behalf of the consortium.[35]

Any lingering uncertainties on the part of either Lutherans or Catholics in Europe and Ethiopia about excluding World Vision from the new partnership were swept aside when an international press release was issued in Holland on October 26. A spokesperson for World Vision announced an agreement with the Ethiopian government authorizing foreign planes to enter the country to deliver food to areas otherwise difficult to reach. According to the announcement, this agreement was part of a larger plan initiated by World Vision, whereby a consortium "composed of five big aid organizations of Christian orientation," namely, World Vision, Catholic Relief Services, Lutheran World Federation, Ethiopian Catholic Secretariat, and Christian Relief and Development Association, would form "a large-scale sea, land, and air bridge of food to Ethiopia" during the coming twelve months.[36] The announcement was based on private negotiations by Dr. Thomas Houston, World Vision president, with Commissioner Dawit of the RRC.[37] Houston had conducted these negotiations without the knowledge of the other partners who, at the same time, were working with World Vision representatives in Addis Ababa on the aims and goals of the consortium.

Two days later, reacting to World Vision's announcement, representatives of CRS, LWF, CI, and WCC in Geneva reaffirmed that further participation by World Vision in the Ethiopia program would not be acceptable. On October 29 the Coordinating Committee of CDAA formally approved a resolution endorsing a coordinated program "to enable the effective implementation of aid which is becoming available." Referring to the Ethiopian consortium, the resolution stated, "It has been decided that they will maintain the traditional partnership." Since the "traditional partnership" was limited to the churches and their related agencies, World Vision was effectively excluded.[38] Its relief programs in Ethiopia, however, continued to operate independently.

Aims and Objectives of CDAA/E

To distinguish the new Ethiopian partnership from the initial Ethiopian consortium, JCAFR, which had included both World Vision and CRDA, members of the Geneva-based CDAA encouraged the adoption of "Churches Drought Action Africa/Ethiopia," or CDAA/E, as its official title.[39] The proposed name change created an identity problem for the partnership more difficult than the one it was intended to solve.

After the message that excluded World Vision from the renamed Ethiopian consortium reached Addis Ababa, the membership was still further reduced by the withdrawal of the CRDA. Since World Vision was also a member of CRDA, its director, Brother Augustine O'Keefe, did not feel he could remain in the new partnership.[40] Representatives of the remaining four partners continued to meet separately at the offices of ECS and LWF in Addis Ababa to complete work on the basic documents. On October 31, at the home of Niels Nikolaisen, they confirmed the new partnership and, as Geneva had suggested, identified it as Churches Drought Action Africa/Ethiopia, CDAA/E. Father Stephanos Tedla represented ECS; Dr. Solomon Gidada, EECMY; Michael Wiest, CRS; and Niels Nikolaisen, LWF.[41]

According to the completed Statement of Aims and Objectives the CDAA/E pledged itself to:

a) Improve worldwide awareness of the nature and gravity of the famine facing the people of Ethiopia.

b) Increase resources for famine relief offered through the NGO sector, to supplement bilateral and multilateral aid being given to the Government of Ethiopia.

c) Support and expand existing NGO famine relief programs and, in consultation with the Relief and Rehabilitation Commission (RRC) of the Government of Ethiopia, establish new programs which will ensure the most effective distribution and utilization of increased food aid.

Member agencies of CDAA/E also were careful to preserve their individual identities and their regular ongoing programs of relief and rehabilitation. For an initial one-year emergency famine intervention program they established an import target of 225,000 tons of food supplies, with an additional request of $40 million to cover costs of port clearance, inland transportation, distribution, and administration, as well as the financing of related medical and rehabilitation needs.

An executive committee made up of the senior executives of each agency would set policy and make decisions for the partnership. A coordinator responsible to the executive committee would handle daily operations through a secretariat composed of experts in food programming and nutrition, budget and finance, logistics, and reporting. Each partner agency would appoint its own coordinator and staff, corresponding to the executive staff of the secretariat.

They agreed that each partner should be responsible for food distribution in assigned geographical areas of the country. ECS would supervise operations in Eritrea, Tigray, Gamo Gofa, and Kaffa; CRS in Gondar, Gojjam, Hararge, and Bale; and EECMY/LWF in Wollo, Shoa, Wollega, Ilubabor, and Sidamo. The United States, the EEC, the Scandinavian countries, Canada, and Australia were expected to be major sup-

pliers of food and funds. To assure accurate accounting for
the handling and distribution of emergency food, the very
detailed and explicit procedures required by U.S. Public Law
480, Food for Peace, would be employed for all imports.[42]

Two sets of written agreements would be required. One
would establish mutual commitments between CRS as coordinator and the individual partners. The other would
regulate relations between the partners and the agencies
cooperating with them in the local distribution of food. It
would be several weeks before a budget and an outline of
working relationships could be completed by the representatives of the partners, and an even longer time before all the
head offices gave their final approval to the documents. But
operations could not wait. Requests for food were already
being prepared, personnel had to be secured, and the machinery for handling the expected influx of shipments had to
be set up.

ETHIOPIA

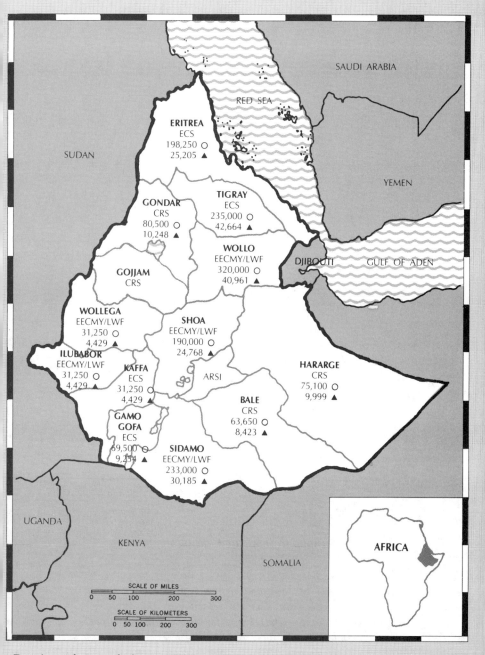

SAUDI ARABIA

RED SEA

SUDAN

YEMEN

ERITREA
ECS
198,250 ○
25,205 ▲

GONDAR
CRS
80,500 ○
10,248 ▲

TIGRAY
ECS
235,000 ○
42,664 ▲

WOLLO
EECMY/LWF
320,000 ○
40,961 ▲

DJIBOUTI

GULF OF ADEN

GOJJAM
CRS

WOLLEGA
EECMY/LWF
31,250 ○
4,429 ▲

SHOA
EECMY/LWF
190,000 ○
24,768 ▲

ILUBABOR
EECMY/LWF
31,250 ○
4,429 ▲

KAFFA
ECS
31,250 ○
4,429 ▲

ARSI

HARARGE
CRS
75,100 ○
9,999 ▲

BALE
CRS
63,650 ○
8,423 ▲

GAMO GOFA
ECS
69,500 ○
9,254 ▲

SIDAMO
EECMY/LWF
233,000 ○
30,185 ▲

UGANDA

KENYA

SOMALIA

AFRICA

SCALE OF MILES
0 50 100   200   300

SCALE OF KILOMETERS
0 50 100   200   300

▲ = Tons
○ = Beneficiaries

Regional Breakdown by Agency, Tonnage and Beneficiaries
(Based on Projections for 1985)

	Tonnage
Ethiopian Catholic Secretariat (ECS)	81,556
Evang. Church Mekane Yesus/Luth. World Fed. (EECNY/LWF)	104,752
Catholic Relief Services (CRS)	28,670
Total: 1,193,499 Beneficiaries	214,978 Tons

"In the days and weeks that followed, Amin's news films, flashed by satellite to 425 broadcasting stations, were seen in millions of homes all over the world. In the U.S. virtually every TV and radio station aired the Ethiopia story."

"One of the most difficult problems facing the partnership was its relation to the Ethiopian Orthodox Church....Meanwhile, Archbishop Jeremiah of the EOC had already expressed to the partners in Ethiopia the desire of the EOC to participate as a full partner in CDAA/E."

VI

The World Discovers
the Ethiopian Famine —————

ON ITS LUNCHTIME NEWS BROADCAST on October 23, 1984, the BBC aired in the United Kingdom the films made by Kenyan journalist Mohammed Amin. On October 24 NBC-TV rebroadcast the Amin films in America. The films finally tore the veil of indifference drawn over Ethiopia and indeed all of Africa. The heart-wrenching scenes and the stirring words of the British narrator Michael Buerck allowed neither governments nor individuals nor TV directors any longer to ignore the Ethiopian tragedy.

Amin's pictures almost did not make it onto American TV networks. An official of NBC News in London recalled the story: "NBC in New York had been offered those pictures by the NBC London Bureau when the NBC London Bureau first knew about them, and the NBC Nightly News show producer had said, 'I have no interest in them at all. Just another famine.' When NBC's London bureau chief, Frieda Morris, and NBC's European news manager, Joe Angotti, saw the pictures on the BBC lunchtime news, they, like everybody else who saw them, were shaken to the core. They phoned New York, to my knowledge, not once but several times, insisting, 'You must run these pictures.' NBC New York's re-ply: 'Thank you. The show is full. We don't have any room for them. Why don't you send them over in an airplane, and we'll take a look at them for next week.'"

The NBC official in London went on: "Finally, Joe and Frieda were passionate enough to get NBC New York to agree to having the pictures satellited into New York from London."

Paul Greenberg, executive producer of NBC's Nightly News in New York, recalled, "Only a few of us were aware that this footage was going to be coming in. The top producers knew it was going to be fed into the news room. But then when it was fed in, the entire news room had access to the monitors and could see what was going on. And, as the footage came over the monitors, there was dead silence in the news room. It soon came over the entire news room that this was a story of enormous magnitude, and that this story was just demanding to be put on the air. We all realized it as we watched it.... Tears came to your eyes, and you felt as if you'd just been hit in the stomach."

The decision was made to put it on the air. Tom Brokaw introduced the segment saying, "For some time now we have been hearing news of another famine in Africa. This time in Ethiopia. Stories of mass hunger and death. But with all else that's going on these days, so often these reports don't have much impact. Words from far-off places. No more. Tonight we end this program with this report from Michael Buerck of the BBC, who went to Ethiopia."

"Dawn — and as the sun breaks through the piercing chill of the night on the plain outside Korem, it lights up a biblical famine. Now, in the twentieth century. Thousands of wasted people are coming here for help. Many find only death. Fifteen thousand children here now, suffering, confused, lost. Death is all around. A child or an adult dies every twenty minutes. Korem, an insignificant town, has become a place of grief. The tragedy, bigger than anyone seems to realize, getting worse every day.... This is Michael Buerck in Korem, northern Ethiopia."

What was regarded as truly newsworthy by the producers of Nightly News on the evening of October 24, two weeks before a presidential election? These items preceded the segment on Ethiopia: (1) President Reagan heckled at the University of Portland; (2) Walter Mondale assails President Reagan's letter commenting on John F. Kennedy's policies; (3) Beirut bombing remembered; (4) special segment on security at U.S. embassies; (5) Grenada medical students honored at the White House; (6) dissenting justice's opinion on the Aquino assassination trial; (7) John Chancellor's commentary on President Reagan's aggressive campaign style.[1]

An Outburst of Compassion

In the days and weeks that followed, Amin's news films, flashed by satellite to 425 broadcasting stations, were seen in millions of homes all over the world. In the U.S. virtually every TV and radio station aired the Ethiopia story. Networks rushed to program interviews and talk shows about the terrible famine; overnight, inquiries and offers of assistance deluged relief agencies. Millions of dollars of cash contributions rolled in.

Beth Griffin, the communications director at Catholic Relief Services in New York, remembers the day after NBC aired the Ethiopian story. The phones at CRS "really started going wild," she recalled. "Between 5 and 9 that evening, we had about a thousand calls." After CRS telephone numbers appeared on one of the New York TV screens, staff members simply laid aside their regular duties to handle the steady stream of calls. TV camera crews besieged the offices, seeking pictures to accompany their stories. Overwhelmed by the offers of assistance, including personal services, clothing, and food of all kinds, the weary respondents finally simply suggested sending checks, which could most effectively be translated into usable commodities or services. The flood of gifts continued to roll into CRS offices in the weeks that followed. By Christmas, 169,878 pieces of mail had been counted. Contributions totaled $23 million.[2]

It was the same story in England, where the Amin films ran consecutively for two nights. The phones rang at Oxfam offices at the rate of four hundred calls an hour. Thames Television technicians suspended a strike long enough to broadcast another Ethiopia film called "Bitter Harvest." The technicians waived their fees and the company donated the advertising revenues to Oxfam and Save the Children Fund.

London's *Daily Mirror* launched its own appeal and sent out a plane the following week loaded with blankets, biscuits, plastic sheeting, and feeding kits. At least four other planes were chartered and offered to Oxfam to carry emergency cargoes.

The Ethiopian authorities also stirred into action. They granted top priority to the unloading and handling of Oxfam's 10,000-ton grain shipment arriving in Assab the week of the broadcast. The British government pledged that a further 6,000 tons would follow. In five days Oxfam received over $1 million in public donations, and by November 6 that amount had more than doubled.[3]

In Holland the national TV network, canceling all other programming, gave over a whole day to telling the Ethiopian story. The Dutch public responded by sending in $18 million for African relief. Their government added $5 million for the transportation of goods to Ethiopia and other drought-affected countries in Africa. These gifts were divided between Catholic and Protestant agencies. In Germany, the agency Brot für die Welt gathered more than $2,500,000.[4]

Even more important than the deluge of actual gifts was the raising of the consciousness of millions of people and the outpouring of compassion for the people they had seen suffering. The outrage felt by these same viewers also exerted a powerful pressure on governments that had moved too slowly or not at all.

Dawit Wolde Giorgis, Ethiopia's Relief and Rehabilitation commissioner, arrived in London five days after the Amin-Buerck broadcast. Unaware of the uproar it had caused in Britain, Dawit stepped off the plane in London to be greeted by a swarm of journalists who fired questions at him about the $150 million dollars his government had just spent to celebrate the tenth anniversary of the Revolution and the 400,000 bottles of whiskey imported from the U.K. to enliven the festivities, while its people were starving. Dawit later confessed that he lied to the press to protect his government — and to ensure his own safety upon returning to Ethiopia. However, he said, his gratitude that the world was finally responding to the needs of his country far exceeded his embarrassment.

Questions were also directed to the British government: Why had it so far done nothing to assist the starving people of Ethiopia? By the time Dawit left London for New York twenty-four hours later, the Royal Air Force was loading two Hercules cargo planes with relief supplies bound for Addis Ababa, and the 6,000 tons of grain pledged less than a week earlier were rushed to waiting ships.[5]

Washington Reaction

With the 1984 presidential election only two weeks away, it suddenly became very important that the Reagan administration demonstrate its concern by sending an emissary to Ethiopia. The State Department managed to delay visa applications for Ethiopia from Jesse Jackson and a Democratic delegation while Peter McPherson, administrator of AID, arranged a hurried meeting with Commissioner Dawit, who had just arrived in Washington. The outcome of the McPherson-Dawit conference was a 50,000-ton grant from AID — the first and only one — directly to the Ethiopian government. That same evening McPherson left for Ethiopia with a seven-person team, even before his arrival schedule or any appointments in Ethiopia had been confirmed.[6]

Circumstances were playing directly into the hands of the CDAA/E leadership in Ethiopia. During McPherson's three-day visit he got a first-hand view of the disaster in Korem and Makelle. At the Hilton Hotel in Addis Ababa he also met with Michael Wiest and Rhonda Sarnoff, regional

nutritionist from the CRS office in Nairobi. They placed
in his hands briefing papers, including a draft of the proposed CDAA/E program and a direct request for 225,000
tons of emergency food, plus $40 million for logistic sup-
port. Rhonda Sarnoff explained the Nutrition Intervention
Program that CRS had been using with great effectiveness
in their regular programs. McPherson, assured before leaving that a detailed plan of operation would be submitted to
AID by December 15, gave his verbal guarantee that the first
50,000-ton shipment would be approved promptly, complete
with full financial support for inland transport.[7]

CDAA/E Goes Public

As reporters and cameramen swarmed into Addis Ababa,
seeking interviews and demanding help for travel to the
famine-stricken areas in the north, agency representatives in
Addis Ababa struggled to complete an outline of procedures
and organization for the consortium. Monsignor Coll arrived
from Rome, bearing the loosely defined but urgent mandate
from CRS/New York to head a CRS Task Force for Ethiopia.
The CDAA/E was to be the instrument through which Coll's
ecumenical mission was to be accomplished. After a quick
look at the structural chart being developed by Peter Lumb,
he put his finger on the coordinator's box and announced,
"This is my job."

Within hours he had arranged a press conference to announce that the CDAA in Ethiopia had been established by a
worldwide network including Catholics, Lutherans, and the
World Council of Churches. Before the week was over he
had visited the top echelons of all the church hierarchies,
including the patriarch of the Ethiopian Orthodox Church,
welcomed the McPherson delegation on behalf of CDAA/E,
located an office site, and ordered business cards and sta-
tionery for CDAA/Ethiopia.

The Ethiopian Catholic Secretariat had just completed
a new building, and Coll arranged with Cardinal Paulos

and Father Stephanos Tedla, ECS executive secretary, for CDAA/E to occupy half the building's ground floor. With the assistance of his new secretary, Elsabeth Samuel, an Ethiopian woman employed by CRS, he arranged for office partitions to be built, telephones installed, and support staff hired. CRS employees looked on with amazement and chagrin as furniture, desks, and typewriters were moved out of CRS offices and moved into the new offices of CDAA/E until permanent furniture could be installed.

Because of the illness of CRS country representative Father Thomas Fitzpatrick, Coll took over his position as well. He met with CDAA/E working committees, received foreign visitors including congressional delegations, and led Mike Wallace and his news team to Bati and Makelle on November 10, where he joined Wallace in interpreting the heart-rending scene shown a week later on "60 Minutes."

The image of CDAA/E that Coll projected in Ethiopia seemed to Peter Lumb, consultant for the design of the partnership, to be the very antithesis of the low-key association intended by the local partners. After twenty-seven years of careful negotiations in the interagency maze of Geneva, Lumb had some reservations about Coll's work style. For his part, Monsignor Coll was determined to get the job done, and the job, as he saw it, was to bring in as much food to Ethiopia as rapidly as possible. Niceties of interaction among the partners, technical questions of shipping and handling, and even concern for nutrition issues were brushed aside in Coll's spirited drive.

His actions raised questions among the agencies associated in the CRDA as to the nature and intent of the new agency. CDAA/E's executive committee therefore asked Lumb to prepare a brief descriptive summary for general distribution, outlining the CDAA/E's proposed structure and program.[8] Terrence Mooney, counselor of the Canadian embassy in Addis Ababa, who served also as chairman of a working group of donor governments, asked for a special meeting with the partnership executives to clarify the sudden withdrawal of CRDA and World Vision from the new association.[9] Finally, representatives of the Ethiopian government found it difficult to understand why, in spite of its high visibility, the CDAA/E had not officially registered and secured the approval of the Ethiopian government.

Among the partners, Father Stephanos, director of the Ethiopian Catholic Secretariat, also had concerns about Coll's style. Stephanos, a strong-minded, energetic personality, active in international Catholic circles, was as an Ethiopian sensitive — not least of all politically — to the presence of a large American agency like CRS in his country. Independently of CRS, through the Caritas network, the ECS was receiving and distributing emergency food, largely from European sources. Probably because these two leaders were so much alike, relations between the Catholic members of the partnership prospered best after both men moved on to other assignments.

The Lutheran members of the partnership enjoyed better internal relations with each other than did their Catholic counterparts. In 1972, the EECMY had invited the LWF, of which it was a member, to assist in responding to an earlier famine. Since that time, the LWF had provided regular financial assistance and maintained supportive service staff in the country. In their dealings with the CDAA/E partnership, the Ethiopian and the international Lutheran counterparts always referred to themselves jointly, as EECMY/LWF.

Solomon Gidada, an Ethiopian who had earned a doctorate from Syracuse University in New York, was the spokesperson for the EECMY. As director for development in his church, he was in charge of relief and rehabilitation programs and strongly supported the cooperative idea. Niels Nikolaisen, an independent-minded Dane, was the in-country representative for LWF. He, too, actively promoted the partnership. Many of the informal discussions leading to the formation of CDAA/E took place at his home outside of Addis Ababa. There the final agreement was reached between the local representatives of the four participating partners on October 31, 1984.

Both Solomon and Nikolaisen shared Lumb's conviction

that the partnership should respect the identities of the participants and their individual programs, and that it should not become a highly profiled agency. Both were sensitive, too, to the strongly American flavor of the enterprise, drawing heavily as it did on the U.S. government for its food supply. Nevertheless, EECMY/LWF remained supportive of CRS's coordinating role.

Crossed Wires

One of the most difficult problems facing the partnership was its relation to the Ethiopian Orthodox Church. During the weeks of October 1984, when the partnership still included World Vision and CRDA and carried the name "Joint Church Action for Famine Relief," the EOC had not been involved. Its absence from these early discussions was due partly to its minimal relief structure, which was focused largely on needy members of its own clergy, and partly to the wariness of the local partners in Addis Ababa regarding the close ties between the EOC and the Ethiopian government. The groundwork for the partnership had therefore been laid without informing the EOC or the WCC, with which the EOC was affiliated. For its part the WCC had taken no initiative either to bring the Orthodox into contact with the developing partnership or to participate themselves.

But when Monsignor Coll arrived in Addis Ababa on November 1 and announced that the consortium was being cosponsored by the WCC, Patriarch Tekle Haymanot of the EOC raised some pointed questions. Since the WCC was a member of CDAA in Geneva, and since the EOC was a WCC charter member, how could the partnership operate in Ethiopia without including the largest church in Ethiopia, with its 20 million members? The Catholics and the Lutherans together, after all, represented only a tiny minority, about one million Ethiopians.[10]

It turned out that Patriarch Tekle Haymanot had sent an urgent cable to the WCC on October 26, announcing the appointment of a national relief committee for Ethiopia and requesting that the WCC relief department become "actively involved in this dramatic situation in the country before it is too late." In the same cable, the EOC had committed itself to provide relief for 140,000 persons, 2 percent of the Ethiopian population affected by the drought.[11]

But the patriarch's appeal had not been shared with other CDAA members in Geneva. WCC representatives had sat silently through the sessions of the CDAA Coordinating Committee on October 29, while Kenneth Hackett of CRS had described the Ethiopian consortium in full detail. Nor was the patriarch's appeal brought to the attention of Brian Neldner, secretary of the Coordinating Committee, until two weeks later. Meanwhile, Archbishop Jeremiah of the EOC had already expressed to the partners in Ethiopia the desire of the EOC to participate as a full partner in CDAA/E and was evidently annoyed with the WCC for not speaking up on their behalf.

On November 12, the acting director of WCC/CICARWS, Dr. George Tsetsis, invited Neldner to meet with Abebaw Yegzaw, the general secretary of the EOC, who had traveled to Geneva to find out what had happened to the patriarch's appeal. Neldner indicated the readiness of CDAA in Geneva to work with the EOC, but pointed out that cooperation in Ethiopia was the prerogative of national church agencies there and not of the CDAA Coordinating Committee in Geneva. Neldner suggested that Abebaw pursue the matter with the churches and agencies in Ethiopia.[12]

Monsignor Coll's generous but unauthorized offer of 30,000 tons of relief food to the EOC shortly after his arrival in Addis Ababa clearly raised false expectations in the EOC and contributed further to a misunderstanding of its relation to the partnership in Ethiopia. Only after extended conversations between the EOC and leaders of the CDAA/E did it become clear to the EOC that an unrestricted allocation of food was not possible under the strict regulations governing the AID grants.

Meanwhile, huge shipments of food and supplies were

virtually on their way. Facilities for unloading, storing, and transporting the food and supplies would have to be ready within weeks. Personnel would have to be ready to receive and handle them. An administrative staff would have to be assembled in Addis Ababa to direct the hiring. Careful planning and bold action were needed.

"Since 1977 CRS had been operating a regular mother-child feeding program in Ethiopia and similar programs in twenty other African countries....The initial grants to CDAA/E were actually an expansion of an already functioning Nutrition Intervention Program."

"By mid-1985, twenty-nine operating agencies had joined the CDAA/E network....In the early months of the program CDAA/E supplied and supervised forty-eight centers throughout the country, concentrated in the most severely affected areas."

"Each team normally would handle approximately 3,600 families per month, or about 18,000 beneficiaries....Since most emergency relief food entering Ethiopia from the U.S. was handled by CDAA/E, it can be affirmed that these shipments reached the people for whom they were intended."

VII

How the Hungry Were Fed ———

ON AN OCTOBER MORNING in 1984, in the village of Wolaita Sodo, four hundred miles south of Addis Ababa, Sister Maura O'Donohue, medical doctor for the Ethiopian Catholic Secretariat, was about to open a new shelter. Hers was the first relief work to be undertaken in this small village. Sister Maura had only a limited supply of food provided by CRS, only a few feeding utensils and medications, and two sisters who worked as her assistants. She later recalled the scene that confronted her that day.

"I have never seen so many hungry people before," she wrote. "At least 3,000 persons swarmed in. We had to go out and line them up in rows and get them to sit. We were desperate — we walked up and down and selected possible survivors to be recipients. I have never experienced anything like it. Adults had kwashiorkor* — such a rarity that it is not reported in medical books. Usually children get it. Ten-to twelve-year-old children were also suffering from the disease. We gave them high-protein biscuits. I have never seen cases so severe."

Sister Maura's experience was by no means unique. Similar scenes were occurring throughout Ethiopia. TV broadcasts

---

*Severe malnutrition, marked by anemia, distended belly, depigmentation of skin and loss of hair or change in hair color.

and press reports documented the tragedy that was costing hundreds of lives every day. Such frantic scenes became the hallmark of the Ethiopian famine and the standard image of the methods employed in famine relief.

Less dramatic, and hence less well documented, were the follow-up methods employed when survivors were able to return to their homes and begin the long process of rehabilitation. Six weeks later, Sr. Maura reported that her program was reaching people in thirty-nine *kebeles* — rural districts, resembling townships. At least ten times more people were being reached through the use of family "take-home" rations. Carefully kept statistics demonstrated that the number of deaths fell drastically, and that the incidence of disease declined.[1]

Nutrition Intervention Program

CRS had used the family "take-home" system successfully during the Sahel famine in the 1970s in Mauritania, Senegal, Burkina Faso, and to some extent, in Togo and Ghana. One of the great advantages of the "take-home" ration was that it allowed children to remain with their families and encouraged families to remain in their villages, thus preventing the displacement of large populations or the congregating of thousands of people in camps around relief shelters.

The philosophy and structure of the program was developed by Father Carlo Capone, during his service as CRS medical director for Sub-Sahara Africa. His findings were codified in a series of field bulletins that were modified for use in Makelle, in Ethiopia, by CRS nutrition specialist Rhonda Sarnoff as early as 1982 and 1983.[2]

Among the six million Ethiopians reported to be in danger of starvation as early as 1983, some groups were more vulnerable than others. CRS had identified children under five years of age and their mothers as the vulnerable group most deserving of assistance and had initiated a food and nutrition program modified to include other members of the family. This modified program, adopted by the CDAA/E partners, was called the Nutrition Intervention Program.

Since 1977 CRS had been operating a regular mother-child feeding program in Ethiopia and similar programs in twenty other African countries. Resources for these programs came from the U.S. government's Food for Peace program, under Public Law 480. The initial grants to CDAA/E, therefore, were actually an expansion of an already functioning Nutrition Intervention Program.[3]

The partnership's local resources included a structure well-suited for a family-oriented food distribution program. Not only were churches and church agencies committed to the nurture of families and children, but Lutheran and Catholic parishes, schools, and medical facilities throughout the country already constituted an indigenous infrastructure for food distribution. As established national churches, Lutherans and Catholics could carry on their relief programs without fear of expulsion by the government, an advantage not shared by many foreign-based agencies.

Focus on the Family: The "Take-Home" System

To implement a selective program of this kind, a great deal of information was needed concerning the number and distribution of people affected by the famine. Famine conditions were not uniform throughout the country, nor was the population evenly distributed. Fortunately, a remarkable amount of data was available through the government's Relief and Rehabilitation Commission, which regularly monitored crop prospects and production and published periodic reports identifying the areas of the country in which food shortages would be most severe. By correlating these reports with population data, the RRC prepared quite accurate estimates of the numbers of people suffering from food shortages.

To ascertain the number of needy families with children under five years of age, each CDAA/E partner resorted first

84   HOW THE HUNGRY WERE FED

to its parishes and institutions, where pastors, priests, and
social workers were sensitive to community needs. In areas
where this was not possible, they contacted community leaders in the networks of *kebeles*, *awrajas*, and peasant associations throughout the country.

The basic principles and procedures for the Nutrition
Intervention Program, as finally put into operation by the
CDAA/E, were developed by a team of professionals representing each of the partner agencies. Members of this team
were Nancy Fronczak, food aid coordinator for LWF, an
American nurse; Dr. Hanne Larssen, medical coordinator for
LWF, a Norwegian physician; Almaz Fiseha, food and nutrition supervisor for CRS; Rhonda Sarnoff, regional nutritionist
for CRS; and Brother Gregory Flynn, head of the Welfare
and Development Department of the Ethiopian Catholic Secretariat. The handbook they prepared described the criteria
for establishing program sites, procedures for staffing, and
guidelines for operating each of the four parts of the Nutrition Intervention Program.[4]

Families with children under five years of age were primary targets of the "take-home" program. This phase of the
relief effort aimed to provide an average family of five persons with a minimum survival ration of 1400 calories per
person per day. The assumption was that the family was either receiving relief from some other source, probably the
RRC, or had some limited food resources of its own, and
that this was therefore essentially a supplementary ration.

Distributed on a monthly basis at a designated distribution center, the ration consisted of two sacks of processed
cereal (soy-fortified sorghum grits), weighing 45.36 kg. or
100 pounds, 4 kg. (8.8 lbs.) of non-fat dried milk, and
one tin (3.6 kg. or 8 lbs.) of edible vegetable oil. The total monthly "take-home" ration for a family of five weighed
52.96 kg. or 116.5 pounds.

The effectiveness of this ration was evaluated by monitoring the growth of the child or children under five years of
age. The intervention team checked such growth when the
family received its monthly ration. According to the calcula-

tions made by the CDAA/E programmers, 200,000 families, or 1,000,000 persons, would benefit from this program.

As individual families registered at the center, each of the children in the family was examined and measured for weight and height (or length). If, according to accepted norms of the relationship between weight and height, a child was found to be less than 80 percent of the established norm, the child was assigned to the "on-site" feeding program. For those children, cooked food was prepared at the center and the child was fed four times each day. Mothers of children who could not attend by themselves also received food at the center, in addition to the regular monthly "take-home" dry ration.

Using special recipes for cooked food, including non-fat dried milk, sugar, edible oil, and corn soy milk, a single ration would supply the child an average of 1800 calories per day. An estimated 58,000 children were expected to participate in this program over the course of a year. An additional 75,750 children who were at 80 percent of the weight/height norm, but who were eating poorly or were lethargic or were not gaining weight regularly, were also provided "on-site" rations, but at a slightly lower nutritional level.

In the event the number of children falling below the 80 percent level became too large to handle, or if their families lived too far away and could not stay on site to permit the children to be fed each day, special arrangements were made. The mother was given a bag of "pre-mix" to take home, containing the same ingredients used for the on-site ration. She was instructed to mix a daily portion with boiled water for each child at home and to return to the center each week to renew the supply. In such cases the family was also eligible for the standard monthly take-home ration.

In addition to the family groups assisted under carefully controlled nutrition intervention programs, the CDAA/E also served a large group of people classified as "destitutes." Such persons were identified by local authorities as the most needy in the area. Priority was given to families with young children, aged five to twelve, pregnant or lactating mothers, elderly, and individuals who were physically or mentally disabled. The ration for this group was the same as that provided for a five-member family. It would be given to such a family or shared by five individual destitute people. The program anticipated benefiting 510,000 persons.[5]

Distribution Network

In order to know how much and what kinds of food to request from donors, the partner agencies had to estimate carefully the numbers of famine-affected families and individuals they could reasonably serve. The division of the country into geographical areas, with primary responsibility for each area assigned to one of the partner agencies based on the agency services already existing in each area, facilitated this aspect of the overall program. On the basis of an analysis of the number of famine-affected people in these areas and the existing facilities and personnel, the agency directors calculated the approximate number of persons they could serve in each category of the famine intervention program.

Nutritionists calculated the weight of the rations for each category of the program and, by simple multiplication, arrived at the total amount of processed cereal, dried milk, edible oil, corn soy milk, and sugar needed per month and for the twelve-month period for which the request was being made. The Plan of Operation prepared through this process became the rationale for the initial CDAA/E combined request to the U.S. government for 225,000 tons of food.

As described earlier, the food arrived in Ethiopian ports and was transported by truck or rail to designated primary distribution points, where it was placed in temporary storage. Smaller trucks carried specific amounts of each food item to the secondary distribution points. Food recipients came to these centers for monthly "take-home" rations or on-site feedings.

At the secondary centers the food became the responsibility of the partner agency in charge of the area: either

EECMY/LWF, ECS, or CRS. Each of these agencies, with the assistance of the CDAA/E coordinator in Addis Ababa, identified and approved the distribution centers and supervised their supply and operation. Many of the centers were housed in church or community facilities. Some were already in operation when the CDAA/E program began, having been supplied through the emergency feeding program begun by CRS in 1983, or through food grants from Europe, Canada, or Australia, channeled through LWF or the Caritas network. As more food became available to the CDAA/E program through AID and other donors, new centers were added.

In the rapidly changing situation in Ethiopia, pockets of need often seemed to appear spontaneously. Susan Barber, relief coordinator for CRS when the CDAA/E program was being set up, recalled the way some new centers were established. "We didn't have to seek them out," she said. "They decided themselves. For instance, a group of volunteers was running an orphanage in Wollo. One day they got up and saw literally thousands of people outside the orphanage. And they said, 'Oh, my God! What are we going to do with these people?' They came to us in Addis and said, 'Look, it's terrible here. We run an orphanage, but we have an obligation to look after people.' So they asked for help. We arranged to send in food and a nutritionist.... Always there was more need than there were supplies."[6]

Among the groups that became affiliated as distributing agencies with the CDAA/E network in late 1984 and early 1985 were Norwegian Church Aid, Concern, Jesuit Relief Services, Save the Children Fund (U.S.), Seventh-Day Adventists, and the Society for International Missions. By mid-1985, twenty-nine operating agencies had joined the CDAA/E network. Each of these participants agreed to the terms and conditions for the use of PL-480 Title II commodities as prescribed by AID regulations.[7]

In the early months of the program CDAA/E supplied and supervised forty-eight centers throughout the country, concentrated in the most severely affected areas. Including satellite distribution stations with limited staff, the num-

ber exceeded one hundred. During the years of the famine and drought, conditions in the country varied; some
areas improved, others deteriorated. Coordinators for each of
the partners watched these changes carefully. Centers were
closed and new ones opened, according to need. This was
also important in order to conserve personnel and equipment. Regular lists were maintained, indicating which centers
were operational at any given time.

Allocations of food were made to the active centers on
the basis of an assessment by CDAA/E staff that need existed and that the agency operating the center was conducting the program in accord with established programmatic,
administrative, and accountability standards. No block grants
of food were made to agencies. Administrative review was
conducted on a center-by-center basis.

Susan Barber described the concern for careful administration of the food grants. "We collected statistics based on
our experience — data gathered at various distribution points:
mortality statistics; how many people died; how many kids
got better; the use of growth charts. We're obligated by the
U.S. government to be responsible for the food, as someone put it very crudely 'from boat to belly.' It is often said,
'Who deals with the government, steals.' That was not true.
The people were getting the food. When people are dying in
front of you, nobody's going to steal."[8]

Staffing the Centers

The effectiveness of the Nutrition Intervention Program depended on knowledgeable and caring distribution center
staff. They faced life and death situations on a daily basis.
For each center a team had to be assembled and trained: a
center manager, a nutrition/health person, a team leader, a
registrar, a weigher, two food distributors, and ten kitchen
workers. The local implementing agency was responsible
for assembling the team, using local people whenever possible. The supervising agency employed specially qualified

personnel, usually nurses or other health care professionals, as trainers. The coordinating office of CDAA/E in Addis Ababa maintained a staff of three supervisor/trainers who responded to requests from the field to train personnel for the opening of new centers. A five-day seminar was conducted for new teams. One- or two-day refresher courses were scheduled periodically to improve skills. Whenever possible, two or three teams were brought together for training.[9]

Detailed training manuals prepared by professional staff described the general program, the facilities, and the necessary equipment for a distribution center. Procedures for registering families, weighing and measuring children, keeping records, and distributing food were spelled out. Each individual working at the center would thereby become familiar, not simply with the particular duties assigned to him or her, but with the whole operation. Special emphasis was given to the spirit in which team members approached their work, the importance of showing personal concern for mothers and children and treating them with gentleness and understanding.

"Remember," wrote Nancy Fronczak in her instructions to center staff, "for many mothers this is a very hard time. They are tired because they do not have good food. They probably have other children at home who take their energy, too. . . . A big part of your job will be to encourage the mother. Give her special praise if her child is doing well. Help her if the child is difficult."[10]

A Center at Work

Each team normally would handle approximately 3,600 families per month, or about 18,000 beneficiaries. Since the center was generally open twenty days per month, the team could expect to serve about 180 families per day. When a center prepared to begin its services, preregistered cards, numbered and marked with a letter of the Amharic alphabet for a particular day of the month, were given out for distribution to the local community or farmers' association or representatives of the RRC, in accordance with the list of needy families.

People from the same neighborhood or village would receive cards with the same letter and were thus served on the same day. To be sure the families returned on the proper day of the following month, center managers used saints' days as references, since these days were very familiar to the local population. These procedures also simplified the follow-up process and made possible a comparison of needs in different areas.

When the family presented its preregistration card, the names of parents and children were entered in the registration book, and a monthly record of the child's growth was begun. With each successive visit, the children under five were weighed and measured and the data entered on each child's growth chart. By recording the weight/height ratio as a percentage of an established norm of 100 percent, a graph could be plotted which, over several months, would show both rate of growth and relation to the norm. A master chart was also maintained, recording how many children were served each day and their distribution according to percentage levels. Such charts were useful records for comparison with other centers or areas and also for measuring the general effectiveness of the nutrition program.[11]

In a seriously affected area in the province of Wollega in southern Ethiopia, for example, 2,000 families began receiving a family ration in May 1985. At the outset 88 percent of the children registered less than 80 percent of the height/weight norm, and 36 percent less than 70 percent. After two months, during which the undernourished children were supplied with a weekly "pre-mix" supplement to take home, the percentage under 80 percent of the height/weight norm dropped to 62 percent. The group below 70 percent, those most seriously malnourished, decreased from 36 percent to 13 percent.

If a child fell below the 80 percent level, the child and

mother were taken to the nutrition/health person for consultation. If medical attention was needed, it was provided. The child might also be entered in one of the special feeding programs, either "on-site" or "pre-mix." At this point the mother was given careful instructions with regard to the importance of following the procedures that would save the life of her child.

After the mother completed her consultation with the team director or the nutrition/health person, the family was brought to the warehouse where the "take-home" rations were distributed. The three main commodities, cereal, oil, and dried milk, were stored separately. At each station the monthly ration was distributed to the family upon presentation of a metal or wooden token authorizing delivery. The sacks of cereal and dried milk and the tin of oil were loaded on the back of a donkey, if the family was fortunate enough to have one. If not, members of the family shouldered the load themselves and trudged off across the rocky fields or along the dusty roads to their villages or "farms."[12]

The most common meals prepared with these basic ingredients were porridges and *injera*, a large, round, thick pancake-like bread, made of fermented dough, baked on a flat pan. When eaten, *injera* is torn into small pieces and dipped into sauces or used to pick up bits of meat or vegetables. In normal times *injera* is prepared preferably with an Ethiopian grain called *"teff,"* but any basic cereal grain may be used.

The CDAA/E partners recognized that medical care is an integral part of nutritional rehabilitation, and so certain basic medical supplies were made available to enhance the nutrition programs. In a famine situation, however, the most effective medicine is food. The goal of the CDAA/E emergency program was not to cure a wide range of diseases but to save the largest possible number of lives.

All the center teams included at least one health professional, either a nurse or a nutritionist, who dispensed medications appropriate to the diseases common to victims of malnourishment and starvation: diarrhea, skin and eye infections, parasitic invasions, and vitamin deficiencies. The most serious and tragic cases were concentrated in "death camps" such as Bati, Makelle, and Korem, where the world was first confronted by the nightmare of mass starvation on film. As "take-home" feeding and health-related programs spread throughout Ethiopia, the wasted bodies of marasmus victims and the distended bellies of children suffering from kwashiorkor were seen less frequently.[13]

Responsibility for each of the feeding centers rested with a relief coordinator appointed by the sponsoring partner. This person made certain that centers were properly staffed and supplied with the necessary food for distribution. The relief coordinators for ECS, CRS, and EECMY/LWF met together on a regular weekly basis under the leadership of the overall CDAA/E coordinator. After the reorganization of the general secretariat in May 1985, the coordinator combined responsibility for managing the CDAA/E office with programming and allocating food to the network of distribution centers. Area coordinators submitted regular monthly reports to the CDAA/E coordinator on the amounts of food distributed and the number of beneficiaries served by each center. The coordinator, in turn, reported to the CDAA/E Executive Committee in Addis Ababa.

Did the Food Reach the Hungry?

Narrative and statistical reports were also prepared by the staffs of each partner agency for submission to their respective headquarters. These reports described both the programs conducted by the individual agency and its participation in the joint emergency program of the CDAA/E.[14]

Of special importance in emergency food programs were reports to donors, mostly governments or international agencies, not all of which required reports as detailed as those demanded by AID. AID's shipments were monitored at every step, from purchase to distribution at a feeding center. Every sack of grain was numbered and counted, when loaded, unloaded, stored, transported, and finally distributed. All losses were carefully recorded. CRS insisted on careful accounting from every agency that shared emergency food grants consigned by AID to CRS on behalf of the partnership.

According to USAID reports, total losses sustained in transporting 358,000 tons of food consigned to CRS in Ethiopia in 1985 and 1986, including all CDAA/E food, came to 4.16 percent. Of this 2.69 percent was damaged or lost during ocean transport and 1.16 percent in Ethiopian seaports. Losses during transport from port to destination under supervision of CDAA/E partners totaled 0.32 percent.

Since most emergency relief food entering Ethiopia from the U.S. was handled by CDAA/E, it can be affirmed that these shipments reached the people for whom they were intended. The same can be said of European shipments monitored by the Lutheran World Federation. More than two million Ethiopians benefited directly from the Nutrition Intervention Program of the CDAA/E.[15]

"The influx of visitors following the dramatic TV broadcasts in late October seemed at times to overwhelm agency personnel. Nevertheless, the visits were recognized as a crucial outgoing channel for information and interpretation."

"Members of Congress went home vowing to back a CRS appeal for an emergency 10,000 tons to fill the gap until the major shipments were cleared for arrival."

"Except for the food allocations, the Ethiopian Orthodox Church continued to operate its general relief program with the direct financial support of the World Council of Churches."

VIII

Launching the Partnership ──────

W HEN THE EXECUTIVE COMMITTEE of CDAA/E convened
for the first time in the offices of the Ethiopian Catholic Secretariat in Addis Ababa, just three weeks after the electrify-
ing TV broadcasts of October 23–24, 1984, many of the basic
elements of the food distribution system were already in operation, though on a very limited scope. CRS was sharing its
limited supply of emergency food from AID with distribution
centers run by the ECS, EECMY, EOC, and several smaller
voluntary agencies. EECMY/LWF had loaned grain received
from European donors to CRS in some especially needy local situations and was cooperating with CRS in its Nutrition
Intervention Program in several localities. Through an airlift initiated by the Caritas network in Europe, 3,000 tons of
grain flown from Asmara to Makelle and other inland centers
was being distributed by ECS in the mountainous interior
where starvation was widespread.

But all these shipments were not enough to halt the influx of starving people to the camps at Bati and Makelle. A
late November telex to CRS/New York reported 25,000 people in the camp at Bati, with 1,000 new arrivals daily. Two
thousand people were receiving emergency feeding twice a
day in an all-too-frequently losing battle for life. Fifty-three

95

deaths were reported at Bati on November 12, and thirty-six more before noon on the following day.

Food supplies in unprecedented amounts were urgently needed. On behalf of the new partnership Kenneth Hackett had already presented a verbal request to the U.S. government for 225,000 tons. As a part of his presentation to the Coordinating Committee of the CDAA in Geneva on October 29, he urged its members to ask for 60,000 tons from the European Economic Community.

On November 13, Brian Neldner, coordinating secretary of CDAA/Geneva, submitted the first request to the EEC on behalf of the Ethiopian partnership for 60,000 tons of emergency food and ECU* 11,700,000 to cover the cost of inland transport. He made the request through the Lutheran World Federation, on behalf of Caritas/Germany, Das Diakonische Werk of Germany, and Danchurchaid of Denmark, all agencies based in countries in the EEC.[1]

At the same time the LWF agreed to ask the Lutheran Church of Australia to request 10,000 tons from the Australian government and to seek an additional 40,000 tons through member churches of the Lutheran World Federation in Germany and Scandinavia.[2]

CRS, with its still limited emergency resources, was under great pressure to assist an increasing number of agencies with food aid. The situation, Monsignor Coll cabled CRS in New York, "is totally dependent on the U.S. immediate approval of the emergency request for 225,000 tons and LWF request of EEC for 60,000. Unless there is rapid approval of these requisitions, we cannot be responsible for consequences."[3]

Leaders and Decision Makers

Under pressures of this kind, the Executive Committee of CDAA/E met for the first time officially to launch the part-

*European Currency Unit, generally equivalent in value to the U.S. dollar.

nership. Seven persons were present at the November 15, 1984, meeting: Tekle Rossario and Brother Gregory Flynn, representing the Ethiopian Catholic Secretariat; President Emmanuel Abraham and Dr. Solomon Gidada, the Ethiopian Evangelical Church Mekane Yesus; Niels Nikolaisen, Lutheran World Federation; Monsignor Robert Coll and Peter Lumb, Catholic Relief Services.[4]

Dr. Solomon Gidada was unanimously named chairman, on a six-month rotating basis. Monsignor Coll, who had been functioning in an executive capacity since his arrival on November 1, was confirmed as coordinator. The structural pattern agreed upon in October had not undergone any basic changes, except that the number of partners had been reduced with the exclusion of World Vision and the withdrawal of CRDA on October 31.

The CDAA/E Secretariat would include four full-time specialists drawn from the staff of each of the partners. CRS would provide food programming, nutrition, logistics, and finance management. EECMY/LWF agreed to assume responsibility for a medical expert and ECS for rehabilitation and development.

The selection process for coordinators for each partner agency was already well advanced. EECMY/LWF announced that their coordinator would be Admasu Simeso, an Ethiopian whose experience had extended into nearly all phases of the EECMY/LWF program since early 1983. CRS designated Susan Barber, an English woman who had served with CRS in Southern Africa and earlier in South Yemen. Abate Getachew, an Ethiopian staff member, became the coordinator for ECS. Both the Executive Committee and the coordinators agreed to meet on weekly schedules, the former to handle policy questions and the latter, operational matters.

Plan of Operation

Before the second meeting of the Executive Committee a week later on November 22, the coordinators met to dis-

cuss the operational plan that would be presented to the U.S.
government in support of the requested grant of emergency
food. Kenneth Hackett, who had initiated both the idea of
the consortium and the joint appeal to the U.S. government,
was present to explain the importance of completing the plan
by December 1.[5]

He emphasized that it must show exactly how CDAA/E
planned to do the job. It must describe how much food was
to be consigned to each port, how the food was to be moved
from the ports to the warehouses or regional centers and
from there to the distribution centers. It must describe the
controls to be exercised and how reporting would be carried
out. The types and quantities of food required and the type
of packaging must be detailed. AID insisted on all this, he
said, in order that emergency food shipments would be re-
sponsibly handled and distributed. CRS was determined to
follow these instructions meticulously to avoid giving Washington any excuse for future delays or cancellations of shipments.

The coordinators gave themselves three days to prepare
the operational plan. Each coordinator would also prepare a
personnel chart and list the methods of transportation, survey, and distribution currently used by their agency. Together
the coordinators would then map out their current agency
programs and their anticipated expansion as required by local conditions. New requests had already been received from
other agencies, including the Red Cross, the United Nations
High Commissioner for Refugees, and the EOC. Concern
was therefore expressed that the existing supply of emergency food might run out before the first large shipment
approved by AID arrived in February 1985.

While the coordinators were at work on these operational plans, the Executive Committee dealt with budgetary concerns and external relations. Interim arrangements
had to be made for covering office expense and personnel costs for the CDAA/E Secretariat. Much of the administrative cost would probably be reimbursed through cash
grants from AID and EEC, in support of food allocations.

A $50,000 advance by CRS provided an immediate oper-
ational resource, and the Executive Committee prepared a
budget requesting each of the sponsoring agencies in Geneva
and New York to supply an initial $250,000 for one year's
operation.[6]

Visitors from Abroad

The influx of visitors following the dramatic TV broadcasts
in late October seemed at times to overwhelm agency personnel. Nevertheless, the visits were recognized as a crucial
outgoing channel for information and interpretation. After
briefings by CDAA/E executives, representatives of governments, the media, and supporting agencies returned home
better equipped to generate support for the massive relief
efforts.

Peter McPherson's visit early in November allowed all
American relief agencies, and CDAA/E, to show a top Washington policy maker conditions in northern Ethiopian camps
and towns that cried out for immediate help. Two Roman
Catholic prelates, Archbishop Basil Hume of England and
Cardinal Alexandre Do Nascimento of Angola, president of
Caritas Internationalis in Rome, paid visits and returned to
Europe to rouse deeper concern among Catholics. Mike Wallace's visit to Bati on November 10 on behalf of "60 Minutes" became the occasion for Monsignor Coll's appeal to
a U.S. television audience. The telecast brought in an estimated $5 million in individual contributions.

In late November a U.S. congressional delegation arrived,
led by Mickey Leland of Texas, one of the earliest and most
outspoken friends of U.S. aid to Ethiopia. He and the other
members of Congress went home vowing to back a CRS appeal for an emergency 10,000 tons to fill the gap until the
major shipments were cleared for arrival in February 1985.
They also assured agency staff that they would press for lift-
ing the prohibition on use of U.S. food in Food-for-Work
projects.[7]

Getting Along with the Government

One of the reasons for structuring CDAA/E as a low-profile partnership of existing agencies was to avoid the necessity of seeking approval from the Ethiopian government through a formal agreement that might impose new restrictions on its operations. In addition, the partners intended CDAA/E as a temporary arrangement, meant to operate only for the duration of the emergency — one year, or eighteen months if the crisis persisted. Agencies, Peter Lumb observed, have an inherent tendency to perpetuate themselves. But the magnitude of the crisis, the aggressive leadership style of Monsignor Coll, the exclusion of World Vision, and the failure to include the EOC as a member of CDAA/E had thrust the partnership into the limelight.

CDAA/E staunchly maintained that it was not a new agency, but simply an arrangement worked out by two indigenous churches and two legally constituted international agencies to increase efficiency and avoid duplication of effort in meeting a great national catastrophe. Nevertheless, the character of the partnership was never fully understood by other agencies, by the U.N., or by the Ethiopian government. The impressive size of its operations and its close ties with AID, by far its largest donor, raised questions in the minds of Ethiopia's Relief and Rehabilitation Commission and a naturally suspicious party apparatus. The questions were aggravated by the U.S. government's decision to provide virtually all its assistance through voluntary agencies rather than through Ethiopian government channels.

Under these circumstances it was incumbent upon the executive leadership of CDAA/E and especially of CRS, under whose longstanding agreement with the Ethiopian government U.S. food entered the country duty-free, to establish and maintain proper contractual relationships with the RRC and its commissioner, Dawit Wolde Giorgis. The commissioner was a man of long experience, both in government and diplomacy. During the early stages of the Revolution he had also served in the military establishment. At one time he had been deputy foreign minister. Appointed in 1983 to head the RRC, his task was to oversee the entire relief operation of the Ethiopian government, both in soliciting a global response to the famine and overseeing the internal efforts at famine relief.

Dawit's dilemma, according to David Korn, U.S. chargé d'affaires in Addis Ababa during the great famine, "was the classic one of officials who try to do good in a system and under a leadership that is inherently bad: one pays for one's license to do some good by making painful compromises with the system and by accepting identification with, and even responsibility for, its more disreputable practices."[8] In the end Dawit found the compromises too heavy a burden, and in 1986, for the sake of his personal safety, chose to seek refuge in the United States.

The RRC, over which he presided from 1984 to 1986, was the channel through which major donations flowed to Ethiopia from the EEC and most other donor governments except the United States. The agency also operated a fleet of several hundred trucks, which transported relief food and supplies to a network of distribution centers in the counties and towns throughout the country.

Unfortunately, on both national and local levels the RRC was subject to the political whims of party functionaries. Nevertheless, the Ethiopian government required that full information concerning food imports and internal distribution plans be approved by officials of the RRC. For this reason CRS and the executives and operational personnel of the partner agencies and of CDAA/E were in frequent contact with Commissioner Dawit and officials in his office.

Bringing the EOC on Board

Relations with the Ethiopian Orthodox Church continued to be a problem for the new Executive Committee. Following the request of Patriarch Tekle Haymanot to the World Council of Churches on October 26 and the visit of Abebaw

Yegzaw to Geneva in November 1984, the WCC sent Teunis van Weelie, former world service director of the Netherlands Reformed Church, to consult with and assist the EOC in preparing a request for aid. Remembering what they perceived as a commitment of 30,000 tons of U.S. food aid by Monsignor Coll, the EOC and its consultant in Addis Ababa worked out a request totaling $23,500,000, including the cost of food and the operation of seventeen centers, and transmitted it to the WCC in Geneva on November 23. The Emergencies Task Force of WCC/CICARWS responded that if the EOC could obtain the food from CDAA/E, thus saving $17 million, the WCC would launch an unprecedented appeal for $7 million to fill the remaining needs cited in the EOC request.

Instead of consulting with Monsignor Coll concerning the appropriate channel for requesting U.S. food, van Weelie went directly to Fred Fischer, USAID officer in Addis Ababa. Fischer advised van Weelie that if CDAA/E would agree to provide for the EOC, USAID would consider increasing the amount of food assigned to CDAA/E. Without further consultation the EOC cabled the WCC in Geneva to put its request on the agenda for the meeting of the CDAA/Geneva Planning Committee on December 10.

When van Weelie finally met with Monsignor Coll, Susan Barber, and Peter Lumb on December 4 to review the EOC request to the WCC in Geneva, he was informed that CDAA in Geneva had nothing to do with requesting food from the U.S. government and that any discussions regarding U.S. government food had to be conducted with CRS, the official representative for CDAA/E. Other features of the EOC request were not compatible with the policies of CRS and its partners, either, especially the EOC plan to assemble food recipients in shelters rather than to use take-home rations. Coll suggested that van Weelie urge EOC personnel to confer with the CRS food programming and nutrition staff.[9]

The CDAA Planning Committee meeting in Geneva on December 10 also failed to convince the WCC representative that WCC membership in the Geneva consortium did not automatically qualify its member church, the EOC, for membership in the Ethiopian partnership. During the visit to Addis Ababa of a pastoral team from WCC December 18–23, the WCC representatives reaffirmed their endorsement of the EOC relief plan based upon a presumed commitment of 30,000 tons of U.S. food through CDAA/E, to be independently distributed through centers operated by the EOC.[10]

Early in January, on the advice of donor agencies meeting in Geneva, the EOC reduced its number of projected centers from seventeen to a more manageable figure and identified four locations in northern Ethiopia: Asmara, Makelle, Ibenat, and Hayk. This led to an understanding on January 29 with CDAA/E in Addis Ababa. Although the EOC was not a formal partner in the consortium, the CDAA/E was willing to cooperate in supplying its initial distribution centers as soon as they were ready to begin a feeding program. In deference to the special status of the EOC, members of the CDAA/E agreed that for the operation of EOC centers, agreements could be signed directly with CRS, irrespective of geographical areas. The CDAA/E Secretariat would instruct the partner agency responsible for Wollo, Tigray, and Gondar to make available the designated amount of food for the EOC centers in those areas.[11]

Except for the food allocations, the EOC continued to operate its general relief program with the direct financial support of the WCC. Some of the supplies for the centers, purchased in Holland by van Weelie, arrived by air in late January. One huge tent was erected in the patriarch's Addis Ababa compound as a training center for EOC relief personnel and for the temporary storage of equipment. In February the four EOC centers were set up, and by April, medical teams from Germany and New Zealand had arrived. CDAA/E trainers continued to give instruction in the Nutrition Intervention procedures and to provide technical assistance as needed. By mid-June of 1986 no fewer than twelve EOC centers were being supplied through CDAA/E with food for 170,000 people.[12]

Lining Up a Working Team

Executives of the partner agencies were eager to have their people in place and their relationships clarified before the massive food shipments began to arrive in the Ethiopian seaports. CRS drew on its experienced Africa field staff, calling in William Rastetter, its country representative in Burundi, to fill the CDAA/E finance post; Robert Roche from Djibouti, as logistics officer; and Ann Hudacek from Togo, to direct nutrition and food programming for CDAA/E, succeeding Rhonda Sarnoff. Although these transfers were made with unusual dispatch, some time elapsed before all were on the job in Addis Ababa. William Rastetter arrived on November 27, Robert Roche on December 9, and Ann Hudacek on January 11. After the major work on the basic CDAA/E documents had been completed, Peter Lumb was persuaded to extend his stay in Ethiopia to serve as first information officer. When Lumb left Ethiopia on March 13, Matthias Schmale, an LWF appointee, assumed the responsibility for preparing official minutes and daily situation reports.

In a move that proved of great importance for the future of CDAA/E, CRS brought in Francis X. Carlin on December 1, 1984, as country representative for CRS and deputy to Monsignor Coll. Carlin was a veteran of twenty years' experience in CRS programs, largely in the Far East: Korea, India, East Pakistan, Vietnam, Indonesia, and most recently the Philippines, where he had served for four years. His appointment provided the managerial experience required to handle the largest single enterprise ever undertaken by CRS. Carlin replaced Father Thomas Fitzpatrick, who had contracted hepatitis during a field trip to the burgeoning camp sites in Kobo in July 1984. Father Fitzpatrick had been compelled to spend several weeks recuperating in Kenya and Seychelles, just at the time plans for the consortium were being developed by Hackett and Wiest.

Carlin's arrival as CRS country representative also resolved some of the structural ambiguity in CDAA/E. He replaced Monsignor Coll as CRS representative on the board of directors of CDAA/E. Coll remained as coordinator of CDAA/E until February 15, 1985, but he was either out in the field or out of the country during much of December and January. In his absence William Rastetter served as office administrator and acting coordinator and after February 15 was asked by the Executive Committee to continue in that capacity.

During December 1984 and January 1985, both the Executive Committee and the coordinators for each of the partners continued to meet on a weekly basis. Finance officers, logistics officers, and nutrition programmers also held regular meetings. By mid-January, management systems for the entire program were in place and functioning. The food/nutrition programmers introduced a nutrition guidelines handbook[13] at a seminar held on January 25. The logistics department produced a field guide for commodity management as a base document for a workshop.[14]

On January 26, Dr. Solomon Gidada, chairman of the Executive Committee, addressed a staff orientation session attended by sixty-five persons, at which he explained the origin and relationships of the CDAA/E. At the same meeting each of the department managers outlined the functions and responsibilities in their areas of work and responded to questions from field staff. On the basis of these final preparations, CDAA/E announced a target date of February 1, 1985, for the formal turnover of all operating responsibilities to each of the partners in their assigned geographic areas.

"None of the partners had ever been involved in a human catastrophe of such proportions. It was to their credit that they realized no single agency could possibly undertake any comprehensive relief activity on its own, as the scattered and fragmented effort of dozens of other well-intentioned groups demonstrated."

"The achievement of the partnership was not that it was conflict-free, but that conflicts were resolved and ways were found to work together in pursuit of a common goal."

IX

Streamlining the Structure ────

WITH THE SIGNING of the official Statement of Intent by representatives of the four partners in Addis Ababa on February 1, 1985, the joint Famine Intervention Program of CDAA/E was formalized. Attached to the statement was a second document entitled "Aims and Objectives and Outline of Working Relationships" describing the mutual obligations and commitments of the partners, worked out since the discussions had begun in mid-October 1984.

A series of agreements, signed on February 4, between CRS and each of the other partners, affirmed their willingness to abide by the conditions established by AID for the handling and distribution of food in their assigned geographical areas. Each partner was expected to sign similar agreements with other voluntary agencies operating within their areas and requesting CDAA/E food for distribution.[1]

From this point on, the Ethiopian Catholic Secretariat assumed responsibility for the distribution of CDAA/E food in the provinces of Eritrea, Tigray, Assab, Kaffa, and Gamo Gofa. EECMY/LWF would handle CDAA/E distribution in Wollo, Shoa, Sidamo, Wollega, and Ilubabor. In addition to serving as the consignee of all U.S. government food, CRS accepted responsibility for Hararge, Bale, Gojjam, and Gondar. All fourteen provinces of the country were covered.

Learning to Work Together

This so-called turnover of responsibilities to the individual partners brought to a close the first, or organizing, stage in the evolution of the CDAA/E, the brief four-month period from October 1984 to February 1985. Given the rush of events that occurred during that time, it is astonishing that documents as cogent and orderly as those of the CDAA/E could have been drawn up and approved by persons and agencies representing three different continents, cultures, and traditions. One of the leading actors described this as nothing less than a "miracle." That the partnership came into being and survived, he said, "with the mix of personalities and all the attendant problems and suspicions is to me a sign of only one thing: God's grace and presence in the midst of it. He made it work."[2]

Part of the problem was that the partnership was not really a partnership of equals. There were Ethiopian organizations that had Ethiopian concerns. And there were international organizations that had international concerns. One agency, CRS, dealing with a primary donor on a global basis, knew that any decision would have an impact on its other programs. Another agency, LWF, was dealing primarily with donors who had a different approach governed in part by the fact that they were not politically involved in the Horn of Africa as the United States was.

None of the partners had ever been involved in a human catastrophe of such proportions. It was to their credit that they realized no single agency could possibly undertake any comprehensive relief activity on its own, as the scattered and fragmented effort of dozens of other well-intentioned groups demonstrated. Yet the decision of the partners to work together by no means implied that they knew exactly how to handle the problems confronting them. The Nutrition Intervention System of CRS was the one element that had been tried and found effective in dealing with malnutrition. The rest, including structure, procedure, and even the relationships among the partners themselves, was experimental. This was crisis management on a grand scale.

Identity Problems

So it was not strange that some mistakes in judgment were made, that decisions made in good faith occasionally had to be changed, that structure was adjusted to meet changing circumstances. All this was already becoming evident as the CDAA/E made the transition into its second, operational stage.

With its bustling new offices in the center of the city, its burgeoning staff, and its well-publicized program, CDAA/E came to be seen as a super-agency, acting for the U.S. government in dispensing thousands of tons of emergency food for Ethiopia. Actually, it was CRS that had the responsibility for submitting food requests to AID, CRS received the shipments of U.S. food, and CRS was finally accountable for what happened to it. But as long as Monsignor Coll was in charge of both CDAA/E and CRS, the distinction was not easily drawn. His frequently quoted aphorism, "CDAA is CRS," obscured the ecumenical nature of the joint venture and engendered both suspicion and criticism from the Ethiopian government and from the community of voluntary agencies.

As the time approached for the actual operation to begin, some very practical problems had to be squarely faced. Regardless of the image that had been projected, CDAA/E was not a super-agency. It was not an agency at all in any legal sense. It was not registered with the government. It could not legally hire personnel, nor could it grant approvals that would enable staff members to secure housing, visas, or work permits. It could not hold legal title to vehicles or open bank accounts or postal boxes. It was, as its carefully drafted documents stated, simply a mutual arrangement among properly constituted agencies "to coordinate a clearly defined Famine Intervention Program" for a limited period of time.

When Carlin assumed responsibility as CRS country representative on January 1, 1985, it was clear to him that both the image of the CDAA/E and the functions of the coordinator's office had to be redrawn if the partnership were to accomplish its mission. Carlin's primary responsibility lay with the CRS office and programs, but he was also a member of the Executive Committee of CDAA/E.

During the months of November, December, and January, virtually all the food distributed under CDAA/E auspices was drawn from earlier CRS emergency grants from AID. The first shiploads of the initial 53,000-ton allocation from AID were scheduled to arrive in Ethiopia in late February. As he faced these realities, Carlin could also see that CRS had committed its best expertise to the CDAA/E joint program. Of the six international CRS staff in Addis Ababa, four had been assigned to CDAA/E, leaving only Carlin himself and Susan Barber, both of whom were also carrying responsibilities relating to CDAA/E.

If CRS was to fulfil its role as consignee, it simply had to have the staff to handle it. Instead, its key people were sitting in the CDAA/E office, several miles across town, at the mercy of a public telephone system that functioned only sporadically.

When Monsignor Coll returned to the United States on February 15, Carlin wasted no time in confronting the problem. At a meeting of the Executive Committee he introduced a series of proposals aimed at limiting the role of the coordinator and the CDAA/E secretariat by eliminating three positions that had not yet been filled. He announced that both ECS and CRS had requested an extraordinary meeting of the Executive Committee to coincide with an anticipated visit from Kenneth Hackett on February 19–20. Matters for special consideration included the high visibility of CRS and of the U.S. government in the CDAA/E partnership and a proposed new job description for the coordinator.

With the departure of Monsignor Coll, a new coordinator

would have to be found, and Carlin expressed the hope that
the position could be filled by an Ethiopian. Until a permanent replacement could be secured, William Rastetter agreed
to serve as acting coordinator, in addition to his duties as
finance officer for CDAA/E and CRS.[3]

What's in a Name?

When the Executive Committee met on February 19, a committee composed of Brother Gregory Flynn of ECS, Admasu
Simeso of EECMY/LWF, and William Rastetter of CRS was
appointed to prepare an outline of options and implications
for the future of the partnership. Their work centered on
two major issues: (1) The name of the partnership and its
implications for relationships with Geneva, the Ethiopian Orthodox Church, and the Ethiopian government; and (2) the
size and function of the CDAA/E Secretariat.[4]

Ever since it had been adopted in late October, the name
"Churches Drought Action Africa/Ethiopia," or CDAA/E,
had created confusion for some and annoyance for others.
All the members felt the partnership should be recognized as
an outgrowth of local initiative, rather than as the auxiliary
of a European-based consortium. The CDAA name had been
suggested by Europeans to emphasize the churchly character
of the association and to relate its activities to the Africa-
wide efforts of the Geneva-based CDAA.

However, use of the name had created the impression
of a much closer relationship than actually existed between
CDAA in Geneva and the Ethiopian partnership. Some felt
that a change of name might remove that confusion and also
quiet complaints that the partnership had improperly appro-
priated the name of the Geneva consortium. This charge
had been voiced by Ludwig Geissel, chairman of the CDAA
Coordinating Committee, during a visit in Ethiopia in early
February on behalf of the WCC.

The use of the name CDAA/E, which in no way identified the membership of the partnership, had conveyed the

impression in Addis Ababa that a new agency had been
created. Individual members of CDAA/E were well-known
to the Ethiopian government, but the aggressive activity of
this new entity, strongly associated with the U.S. government, even suggested to the Ethiopian government a possible subversive intent, especially since its leaders denied that
they were an agency and declined to register as such with
the RRC. The apparent exclusion of the Ethiopian Orthodox
Church from membership raised further questions within the
Ethiopian political party structure about the CDAA/E's close
ties with the U.S. government.

Serious consideration was therefore given to dropping the
name, even though it was recognized that a sudden change
might convey the impression of instability and might also
jeopardize the partnership's position with the governments
to which requests for food had already been addressed. As
a replacement, the original name of the consortium, "Joint
Church Action for Famine Relief," was suggested. Another
option was to incorporate the names of all the member agencies, to remove any impression that a new agency was in
operation.

The issue of a name was more than cosmetic. It involved
the identity and character of the entire venture. Particularly
during the early months of 1985 it became a problem of sufficient magnitude that efforts were actually made to avoid
the use of any name at all. The official CDAA/E letter-
head, calling cards, and logo prepared by Monsignor Coll
were withdrawn, except for restricted internal use. All official
correspondence was signed, not by the coordinator, but by
the executives of all four member agencies and was stamped
with their individual agency seals.

In some respects the role of the secretariat was an even
more critical issue than the name of the partnership. Its size
and location gave credence to claims that CDAA/E was indeed an operating agency and that it should, therefore, seek
official recognition by the Ethiopian government. Commissioner Dawit, who was generally supportive of the work of
relief agencies, confronted the executives on one occasion

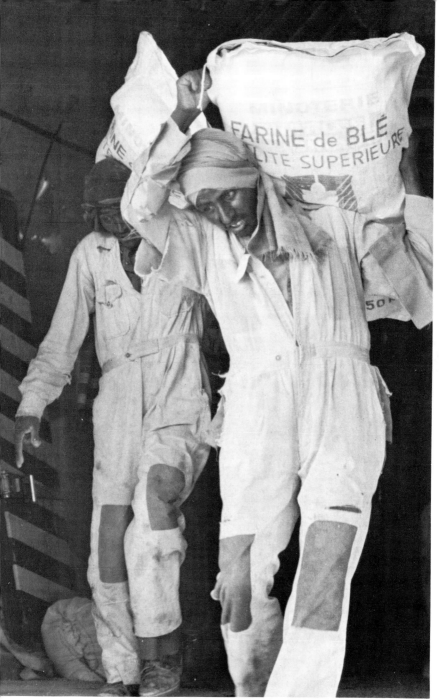

Ethiopian workers unload a shipment of food at the airport in Makelle.

Workers gather around a new shipment of food in Korem, Ethiopia.

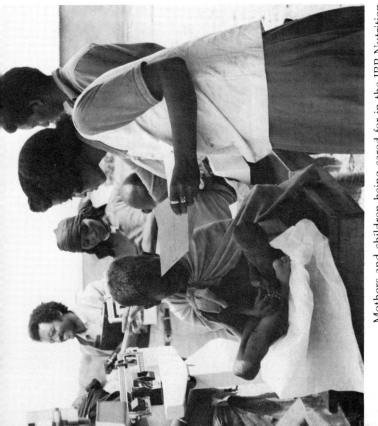

Mothers and children being cared for in the JRP Nutrition Intervention Program in Ethiopia.

The work of Joint Relief Partnership goes on. Shown below is a driver under JRP auspices (note shield on truck and shirt) just returned from delivering food to Tigray.

A food relief truck convoy in Dessie, Ethiopia, awaiting permission to continue to deliver food to drought victims.

Warehouses in Dessie where stored food is being loaded on trucks for delivery in remote regions.

Mother and child (above) and group of men (below),
victims of drought, await life-sustaining food distributions.

Three women wait for food at the food distribution center in Korem.

Father and child, drought victims, await their food allotment in Korem.

Orphaned children at food distribution center in Ethiopia, during the 1984-85 famine. These children have since been reunited with their family.

All photos in this section, except of the Nutrition Program, are by Betty Press, Photographer, Africa Photos, Nairobi, Kenya.

with the outline of the CDAA/E structure, complete with six departments and appropriate supportive personnel. Embarrassed, the executives responded that they did not see the partnership as an established agency, but simply as a means for the four agencies to coordinate their efforts during the duration of the crisis. They referred the Commissioner to the Statement of Intent and the document on aims and objectives, which stated these intentions clearly.

One way in which the partners could show they meant what they said was to scale down the size of the secretariat and place more specific limits on the functions of the coordinator. Another action would be to move the secretariat from the ECS building to smaller quarters commensurate with a reduced staff and function.

The extraordinary meetings of the Executive Committee on February 19–20 pointed to basic changes in the structure of the partnership. Kenneth Hackett, representing CRS leadership in New York, attended the meetings. At their conclusion he cabled Pezzullo that in keeping with the original concept of the partnership, he felt it was time for the functions of the CDAA/E Secretariat to revert to the partners. While the identity of each partner should be maintained, the "logistic, financial, and nutrition programming unit should be placed under one executive agency, probably, but not necessarily, CRS."[5]

The Steering Committee of CDAA, meeting in Geneva on March 11, also called for the scaling down of the size and function of the secretariat, for the reduction of its administrative budget, and a change of name.[6]

When Peter Lumb, one of the architects of the original plan of operation, prepared to leave Ethiopia on March 13, he incorporated in a letter to Kenneth Hackett his own formula for restructuring. He supported Carlin's proposal to reduce the sections of the partnership from six to four: logistics, finance, food/nutrition programming, and information. He favored a new and more restrictive job description for the coordinator. As a replacement for the name, CDAA/E, he suggested "ECS, EECMY/LWF, CRS Joint Program for

Famine Relief," or in a shortened version, "Joint Program."
A general public statement would explain that the CDAA/E
name and logo had been employed in order to facilitate the
launching of the program and could now be replaced by a
more descriptive title. Lumb also recommended keeping the
RRC more fully informed of Joint Program activities.[7]

Internal Growing Pains

During the critical reevaluation of CDAA/E in February and
March, both Dr. Solomon Gidada and Niels Nikolaisen were
out of the country, Nikolaisen on leave, and Dr. Solomon
traveling in the United Sates and Europe. While their views
were generally represented by Dr. Emmanuel Abraham and
Admasu Simeso, the official counsel of the two executives
was not available and the decision-making role of the Executive Committee was therefore limited. No regular meetings
of the Executive Committee were held during the month of
March. Francis Carlin, in turn, spent much of the month of
April at CRS headquarters in New York.

At the May 3 CDAA/E Executive Committee meeting in
Addis Ababa, Carlin reported on the situation that had developed regarding the payment of inland transport costs by
the U.S. government. On the basis of past experience, CRS
had assumed that in emergency situations AID would pay
the full cost of transporting food from Ethiopian ports to local distribution centers. In early February, however, AID had
begun pressing voluntary agencies to pay 50 percent of these
costs. Carlin's report and his stated expectation that the partners would have to share these costs generated apprehension
among ECS and EECMY/LWF staff members.

Even more disturbing was Carlin's announcement that for
internal reasons William Rastetter and Robert Roche, CRS
staff assigned to CDAA/E for finance and logistics, would
now be relieved of all CDAA/E functions.[8] Although he assured the committee of the continuing commitment of CRS
to the partnership and his readiness to provide Ethiopian na-

tionals to fill the vacated positions, Carlin's announcement seemed to lend some credence to the persistent rumors that the CDAA/E Secretariat might be absorbed by CRS. In a sharply worded position paper, EECMY and LWF reacted to Carlin's announcements, questioning whether withdrawing Rastetter and Roche would in effect dismantle the secretariat and possibly the partnership itself.

Such sharp words from the usually soft-spoken and diplomatic Dr. Solomon reflected both his disappointment and his resentment. He acknowledged that the initial successes of the secretariat in coordinating field and finance operations were largely the work of personnel assigned to CDAA/E by CRS: Roche, Rastetter, and Hudacek. Their past experiences with U.S. food procedures were essential to the operation and could not be replaced on such short notice. The paramount concern of the EECMY/LWF executives, however, was that "this first-time joint effort by Catholics and Lutherans on such a large scale" must not fail but come through to be seen as "a model for future emergency situations."[9]

In the days before the next regular meeting of the Executive Committee on May 8, acting coordinator William Rastetter felt the tension serious enough to poll all the individual executives on their attitudes toward continuing the partnership. When the meeting opened, Rastetter was able to announce a consensus, and the partners individually reaffirmed their commitment to their common mission.

They then turned to the task of reconstituting the secretariat and the coordinator's office, restoring them to the more modest dimensions originally intended. Committees composed of the logistics and finance officers for each of the partners would replace the full-time CDAA/E logistics and finance officers. The nutrition section of CDAA/E, under Ann Hudacek's direction, remained unchanged, except that necessary clerical support staff was added. Dr. Hanne Larssen continued as the medical coordinator and Matthias Schmale as the information officer for both CDAA/E and for EECMY/LWF.

A new job description was authorized for the Office of the coordinator, limiting its function to office administration and liaison between the Executive Committee, the new functional committees, and the coordinators' committee, over which the CDAA/E coordinator would preside. Ann Hudacek was asked to add the position of acting coordinator to her responsibilities for nutrition programming. Before William Rastetter resumed full-time work as finance officer for CRS, he was asked to prepare an "organogram," setting forth the revised CDAA/E office structure.[10]

Tensions and conflicts such as these among the partners were infrequent but real. Some were rooted in personality differences, some in cultural differences in style and pace of decision making. All were in some way related to the climate of crisis in which decisions had to be made. The stakes were high. It was essential to act. Thousands of people were starving, and for them even the prosaic procedural decisions of a committee might make the difference between life and death.

The achievement of the partnership was not that it was conflict-free, but that conflicts were resolved and ways were found to work together in pursuit of a common goal. In reviewing events just past, Francis Carlin observed that this unity had been tested a number of times, but that with their mutual recommitment, the partnership had probably survived its most serious test. Dr. Solomon's precept had been honored: "Whatever we do should be aimed at helping the people of Ethiopia."

"People continued to stream into the camps. The CDAA/E reported that there were seven camps in the Makelle area with a total population of 75,000, and 20,000 more were waiting to get in. In March, fifty to sixty persons died every day."

"Many peasants were dismantling their homes to sell the wood and grass to buy food. The dismal scene of people tearing down the last symbol of the land they had populated so long seemed to one reporter the ultimate symbol of despair."

"At the same time, United Nations and Ethiopian government appeals to the governments of the world began to bear fruit, and thousands of tons of food and other relief commodities started arriving in Ethiopian seaports."

X

Keeping the Wheels Turning ——

THE MONTHS FROM FEBRUARY TO JULY 1985 were probably the most critical in the life of the Ethiopian partnership. Famine conditions were at their worst. The failure of the late rains of 1984 had brought the northern provinces of Tigray and Wollo to the brink of hopelessness and despair, while the scourge of hunger spread into the central and southern provinces of Shoa and Sidamo. Total grain production of the country in 1984 was 25–30 percent lower than in the previous year, also a disaster year. Estimates of persons needing assistance in this country of 42 million rose to 7.75 million.

People continued to stream into the camps in Tigray, Wollo, and Gondar. The CDAA/E Information Service reported that there were seven camps in the Makelle area with a total population of 75,000, and 20,000 more were waiting to get in. In March, fifty to sixty persons died every day. From February 10 until the end of March, no food convoys were able to reach Makelle because of the military action in the area. Flying over the fighting might have helped. But due to a fuel shortage even the airlifts were temporarily curtailed.

In Gondar the camp population at Ibenat reached 45–50,000, with thousands of others living in open fields. Sanitation was poor, and medical conditions were aggravated by the sudden influx of even more starving people.

In northeastern Shoa the RRC had to open a new camp at Bettie. Many peasants were dismantling their homes to sell the wood and grass to buy food. "The dismal scene of people tearing down the last symbol of the land they had populated so long" seemed to one reporter the ultimate symbol of despair.[1] Even if the rains came during the next several months, there would still be no harvest until October. Until then and well beyond, disease and starvation would continue to create havoc throughout the land.

Floods of Food at Last

The distribution network of the CDAA/E partnership went into high gear, directing the flow of food through sixty-five centers in ten of Ethiopia's fourteen provinces. During February and March, its first two months of official operation, the partnership drew upon 32,559 tons of food supplied to CRS by the U.S. government under an earlier emergency grant approved in November 1984, but not delivered until 1985. It also dispensed 15,150 tons of food shipped from Finland and Sweden to the Lutheran World Federation. During the month of March the CDAA/E network provided food for 1,349,275 persons. More than 266,000 family groups received "take-home" rations and more than 60,000 malnourished children "on-site" enriched rations.[2]

Up to March 31, 1985, only 9,000 tons of the 225,000 tons requested by CDAA/E from AID in November 1984 had reached Ethiopia. None of the 60,000 tons requested from the EEC had yet been approved. Then, during the months of April and May the pipeline from America to Ethiopia, from AID to CDAA/E, began to flow. By the end of May 40,000 tons had arrived. By July 1, 65,000 tons were on hand, and the rest of the 161,000 tons thus far approved by AID was scheduled to arrive in monthly shipments through September. After extended delays, the EEC approved a grant of $7 million to be used for the purchase of grain and the payment of inland transport costs. Approximately 10,000 tons was scheduled to reach Ethiopia in August and September 1985.[3]

At the same time, United Nations and Ethiopian government appeals to the governments of the world began to bear fruit, and thousands of tons of food and other relief commodities started arriving in Ethiopian seaports. Grain ships had to wait days to unload their cargoes in Assab and Massawa, Ethiopia's two ports. Neither they nor the neighboring port of Djibouti, which transshipped a small portion of the food to Addis Ababa by rail, was equipped to handle such heavy traffic. Grain shipments overflowed the limited warehouses and piled up on the docks. On April 1 it was reported that 100,000 tons had accumulated in the port of Assab alone, including 20,000 tons of CDAA/E food.[4]

Relief agencies complained repeatedly to the RRC, and finally, on May 8, Kurt Jansson, U.N. relief coordinator, was able to induce Lt. Col. Mengistu himself to visit and inspect the port of Assab. As a result of his visit, the "off-take" at Assab increased from about 1,500 tons to 3,000 tons per day. Ann Hudacek, CDAA/E coordinator, recalled May 4 as the day a freak rainstorm in Assab destroyed several thousand tons of grain piled up on the docks, waiting to be bagged.[5] Clifford May's article in the *New York Times* on May 17, "In Ethiopia Food Rots on the Docks," detailed the loss, but also pointed out that the pile-up of food on the docks was not due to agency neglect, but to inadequate port facilities and lack of trucks to move the food.

The Great Truck Shortage

Kurt Jansson of the United Nations asked donor nations for $50 million worth of new trucks, tires, and spare parts to be used to transport food. If this equipment was not received within the next three months, he said, "imports of emergency food must be halved."[6]

All voluntary agencies, including the CDAA/E partners, depended heavily upon the 1,400-truck fleet of the National

Transport Corporation (NATRACO), a government-owned operation, with which they contracted for transporting food. Some additional service was available through the Ketena System, a commercial fleet of about 1,600 trucks coordinated by the government, although their rates were often higher than the voluntary agencies were prepared to pay. These fleets, together with the 1,000 trucks operated by the RRC, represented the total nonmilitary trucking resources in Ethiopia, available for both commercial hauling and for the transport of relief supplies.

Since the famine intervention had begun, all voluntary agencies had purchased as many trucks as they could afford, and had included truck purchases in their requests for government funds. At the end of 1985, the partners of CDAA/E were operating a total of 106 long- and short-haul vehicles. The CRDA, though not intended to be an operational agency, had built up a fleet of 66 trucks, which it placed at the disposal of voluntary agencies. The combined trucking operations operated by all voluntary agencies throughout Ethiopia numbered only 621 vehicles.[7]

One of the most imaginative solutions to the transport problem was a contract negotiated by Francis Carlin to lease an entire fleet of trucks from Contrax, a private firm in Nairobi, Kenya. Fifty-five heavy vehicles with a total capacity of 2,000 tons were engaged to operate between the port of Assab and CDAA/E's primary distribution points at Nazareth and Kombolcha. The entire operation was "containerized." For each vehicle three 40-foot, 35-ton containers were provided, one aboard the truck, one at the port, and one at the primary distribution point. A vehicle coming from the port to the primary distribution point with a full container unloaded the container with a heavy-lift crane and reloaded an empty container. The driver then returned to Assab, where he left the empty container and picked up a full one for the return trip. With a "turn-around" time of six days for each trip, the fleet was able to transport 10,000 tons per month.

The containerized operation not only speeded the movement of food but addressed the storage problem as well. CDAA/E food in the port no longer needed to be stacked in the open awaiting transport. Moreover, the contractors also agreed to erect temporary warehouses of 10,000-ton capacity at both Nazareth and Kombolcha. The total cost of $6 million for a nine-month operation, beginning October 1, 1985, was covered by a grant from AID.[8]

AID Reneges on Transport Costs

For the newly-constituted CDAA/E the impending and actual arrival of the first large shipments under the major AID grant produced new tensions with the U.S. government and even strained relationships within the partnership. Who was responsible for the costs of inland transport of the donated food? The usual policy of AID in its regular Food for Peace program was that the U.S. government donated the food and paid the cost of ocean transport and the receiving country paid the costs of local port handling and inland transport. Under emergency conditions like those in Ethiopia in 1983 and 1984, both port costs and inland transport had regularly been covered by the U.S. government. The CDAA/E emergency request for 225,000 tons submitted in January 1985 was based on these expectations.

According to the budget prepared by CDAA/E, the total cost of the project was estimated at $185 million. The U.S. government was asked to provide $130 million, $90 million for the food at $400 per ton, and $40 million for the costs of transport, handling, and administration. Contributions from other international donors for food and transport were estimated at $40 million and private contributions for personnel, facilities, air transport, and trucks at $14 million. The U.S. government was thus being asked to provide 70 percent of the total budget, while other sources would contribute 30 percent.

On the basis of their experiences with previous AID emergency grants, verbal assurances of support by Peter

McPherson, AID administrator, during his visit in Addis Ababa on November 5, 1984, and subsequent conversations with AID officials and members of Congress, CRS anticipated full funding of inland transport and administrative costs. It had established firm commitments with the Ethiopian government and with CDAA/E partners and church officials. Without this fiscal support the operation of the CDAA/E food distribution system would not have been possible.

In late January and early February, however, CRS began to receive indications that AID was changing its position on inland transport funding. In addition to the Ethiopian emergency, AID had also made commitments to a food program in Sudan, which had turned out to be more costly than anticipated. In view of an expected financial shortfall in AID resources, CRS staff members were asked informally what the agency's reaction would be to a formula dividing transport costs. They responded that they believed they had a commitment from the U.S. government for full funding.[9]

By February 1, 1985, the date on which the partners were to take over the management of CDAA/E food distribution in their respective geographical areas in Ethiopia, no official word had as yet been received from AID. With responsibility for distribution of the largest tonnage in its assigned areas, EECMY was especially alarmed at the uncertainty concerning funding of inland transport costs. Admasu Simeso, EECMY/LWF coordinator, repeatedly raised the issue. He reminded CRS of its own earlier insistence that no food be accepted without the assurance of necessary financing of transportation and distribution. Father Stephanos of ECS likewise saw no way that his agency would be able to find funds for inland transport if CRS was unable to secure reimbursement from AID.[10]

At this point, John Donnelly, director of material resources for CRS in New York, took action. On February 11 he addressed a letter to William Pearson, chief of the Title II Food for Peace Office in Washington, and to General Julius Becton, director of the Office for Foreign Disaster Assistance, expressing his deep concern that, although a 53,000-ton allocation of food for CDAA/E had been approved in late November 1984, no support funds had yet been forthcoming. The food itself was now scheduled to arrive in Ethiopian ports between February 21 and April 6, 1985. CRS, he said, had accepted the grant of food in good faith, but was now placed in a position that hazarded its own credibility with its partners in Ethiopia and jeopardized the efforts of CDAA/E to save the lives of thousands of starving people.[11]

The signals from Washington were not promising. Just two days later, on February 13, Lawrence Pezzullo received a letter from Julia Chang Bloch, assistant administrator of the Office of Food for Peace. Making no reference to CRS's request, Bloch's letter set forth a new AID policy on fiscal support for emergency food grants. Financial overview statements, she wrote, would henceforth be required to accompany requests from voluntary agencies, describing the source, nature, and amount of support raised and expended by the agency in the country involved. Of special importance would be a projection of the agency's contribution toward the cost of in-country transportation.[12]

Faced with the options of rejecting the incoming shipments or simply allowing them to lie in warehouses while people starved, CRS leaders undertook to advance the full logistical, distribution, and administrative costs for the 53,000 tons scheduled to arrive in the immediate future, but only with the understanding that it expected reimbursement to follow.

There was no response from Washington to Donnelly's letter. CRS began to advance private funds to keep the food moving, eventually committing a total of $7,600,000. On March 4, AID informed CRS by phone that funding for inland transport of the 53,000 tons had been approved in the amount of $7 million, but that no money for related administrative expenses had been included.

On April 11 the second emergency food allocation of 56,000 tons for CDAA/E was approved by AID, also without support funds. On May 1 the third allocation of 51,387 tons won approval, and AID agreed to fund $3 million against transport costs for the second shipment.

Meanwhile, in late April, responding to continuing public pressures, Congress passed a supplemental appropriation for African relief, authorizing almost $400 million in food aid, including up to $100 million for inland transportation costs, and authorizing additional funds "for emergency relief and recovery assistance for Africa." With these additional resources available, full funding of the CDAA/E program in Ethiopia should have been assured. However, to the chagrin of CRS, AID now made explicit its new cost-sharing policy requiring voluntary agencies to absorb 50 percent of inland transport costs for emergency food shipments.[13]

CRS versus AID

In response to what he regarded as a breach of faith on the part of AID, Lawrence Pezzullo directed a sharp letter to Peter McPherson on May 6, reminding the AID chief that during his November 1984 visit to Ethiopia he had promised full support to the CDAA/E program for distributing 225,000 tons of food during 1985. He reminded McPherson further that when AID had encountered fiscal constraints because of the scope of an Africa-wide food emergency, CRS had advanced its own funds for Ethiopia. But when congressional action had removed those constraints, AID had continued to withhold reimbursement, in spite of verbal assurances to CRS from McPherson's office. Such arbitrary determination of the use of privately contributed funds by government, Pezzullo warned, was not only unfair but also constituted a threat to the viability of private voluntary agencies.

He reminded McPherson that CRS and other voluntary agencies were simply the instruments through which Congress had chosen to implement its program of famine relief in Ethiopia. If the agencies were to fulfill effectively the congressional mandates to deliver food to those in need, AID should provide them with the means to do so.[14]

A few days later, on May 20, Pezzullo and other senior members of his staff met with McPherson in his Washington office. By this time AID had approved a total of 161,000 tons for CDAA/E, but had committed only $10.6 million for support services. During the meeting an agreement was reached whereby $22.5 million, representing the full cost of inland transport at $140 per ton, was committed by AID. AID also agreed to finance fully a $6 million program sponsored by CRS for leasing a fleet of fifty-five heavy-duty trucks from a firm in Kenya.[15]

These understandings were confirmed in a mutual exchange of letters between Pezzullo and McPherson. This same exchange of letters made it clear, however, that the fundamental disagreement between CRS and AID had not been resolved. While acknowledging that the "issues of pressing concern" appeared to be settled, Pezzullo restated the CRS concern that the government's original pledge for full transport funding had been arbitrarily set aside on the assumption that private agencies had received large sums of money from private donors and could therefore assume these costs.

He pointed out that the infrastructure developed by the CDAA/E partners in response to their initial understanding with the U.S. government had made possible the feeding of two million people at a distribution rate of 20,000 tons per month. This system of distribution within Ethiopia would be seriously jeopardized unless the question of who paid the cost of moving food inland from the ports could be resolved. Requests for the new fiscal year were in process of preparation, and the latest estimate from the RRC indicated that five million people in Ethiopia would still require emergency assistance.[16]

McPherson's response confirmed the agreement to pay the full inland transport costs for the 161,000 tons, to fund the Kenyan truck-leasing plan, and also to fund the Northern Initiative, a new program by which CRS agreed to expand its emergency distribution into areas of Eritrea not under government control. But all future requests for emergency food and transport, McPherson said, would have to be evaluated on a case-by-case basis. The concept of "burden sharing" would remain an important dimension of AID's partnership with the private agencies.

McPherson concluded his letter with the hope that "better communication" between the senior CRS and AID offices might prevail in the future and thus prevent any further misunderstandings that might "seriously impede our shared objectives of relieving human suffering in Africa."[17]

An act of Congress passed in late April opened the way to a compromise on the inland transport problem. Part of the Supplemental Appropriations Act made available $137.5 million through the Office for Foreign Disaster Assistance for emergency relief and recovery assistance for Africa. For such disaster-related aid the restrictive Hickenlooper and Brooke amendments to the Foreign Assistance Act of 1961 were lifted, permitting funding of a "food-for-work" program and a variety of rehabilitation proposals by voluntary agencies.[18]

Only a few days later, on May 8, CRS announced its own $50 million Omnibus Program for Africa, using private funds contributed to CRS in the wake of the TV broadcasts in October 1984. Thirty million dollars were earmarked for Ethiopia and $20 million for other beleaguered African countries. Part of the funding addressed emergency needs, including the logistics and operation of feeding programs and the purchase, transport, and distribution of such items as blankets, tents, and clothing. These items were not included in the CDAA/E program, which was limited to emergency food distribution. Other categories were designed to meet short-term development needs in agricultural production, water and sanitation, health and medical services, and income-generating activities. The emphasis in these programs was on improving conditions in camps and hard-hit rural areas and on providing the basic means for victims of the famine to return to their homes and to some measure of productive life.[19]

In announcing this new program, Pezzullo made clear

that the emergency had not yet passed and that continued food aid would also be needed for at least another year. But relief was only a first step. "We must make every effort," he declared, "to move quickly to provide assistance to people to help themselves as soon as possible." The CRS Omnibus projects were meant to stimulate these recovery efforts.[20]

The congressional legislation was not only a substantial additional contribution to Ethiopian welfare. It also removed one of the peculiar twists in U.S. emergency relief policy that had defined food as essential to the fight against famine, but excluded "food-for-work" grants or grants to supply water or seed and tools for recovery.

On June 26, 1985, senior staff of CRS and AID met in Washington to discuss CRS programs for the fiscal year 1985–86. Since CRS had a complete package of rehabilitation projects ready to be implemented in Ethiopia using private funds, it was proposed that AID fund $18–20 million of these projects with public money. In return, CRS would use an equal amount of its private funds to pay half the inland transport costs for emergency food to be approved by AID for the CDAA/E program in 1985–86. AID would fund the other 50 percent of the inland transport costs directly. Both parties agreed not to regard the settlement as either compliance or concession, but rather as a practical way out of a persistent dilemma.[21]

Problems with the Press

Just at this juncture, with relations between CRS and AID under severe strain, a bitter attack on the policies and practices of CRS was launched in the public press. During the summer of 1985 some disgruntled former employees of CRS directed complaints to the U.S. Catholic Bishops Conference concerning alleged irregularities in the fiscal procedures employed by CRS in two African countries. The bishops examined the allegations during their summer conference in 1985 and dismissed them as groundless.

Later in the summer, however, embellished with more general criticisms of the CRS programs in Ethiopia, especially the refusal of CRS to pay the inland transport costs it claimed the U.S. government had promised to pay, James MacGuire, one of the former CRS employees, brought the charges to the attention of the *New York Times*. On August 7, the *Times* published a lengthy story under the headline: "CRS Involved in Dispute Over Spending of Ethiopia Aid."

Moving beyond the earlier complaints submitted to the bishops, *Times* reporter Ralph Blumenthal criticized CRS for having failed to spend properly the substantial amount of private gifts collected since October 1984 as a result of the television announcement of the Ethiopian crisis. Blumenthal asserted that only about $8 million of the $50 million collected had been spent, and that meanwhile CRS had been engaged in a dispute with the U.S. government about who should pay for the transportation of emergency food in Ethiopia. The impression was created that a wealthy relief agency was hoarding resources contributed by the public and allowing people in Ethiopia to starve while it argued with the government over transportation costs.

It was not an easy matter to respond effectively to the charges aired in the *Times*. Lawrence Pezzullo wrote a letter complaining about the handling of information given to the *Times* reporter and stated emphatically that no relief distribution had ever been held up for lack of money to move the food. In fact, he pointed out, CRS had advanced almost $8 million of its own money when the U.S. government had failed to provide funds for this purpose.[22] Following the dramatic pictorial displays of starvation in Ethiopia, it was difficult to explain that the longer-range rehabilitation projects, for which CRS had allocated the privately-donated dollars, were of equal importance with immediate life-saving measures. Complicating the picture even more was the difficulty of explaining to a public that could scarcely locate Ethiopia on a map the special logistical problems in delivering food to the needy.

These attacks on CRS were picked up and repeated in newspapers and periodicals across the country. Eventually, the National Conference of Catholic Bishops appointed a special commission, headed by Cardinal John Krol, archbishop of Philadelphia, to look into the charges. Retaining both an outside accounting firm and a New York law firm, the Krol Commission conducted a thorough investigation in which seventy-five persons in the United States and Ethiopia were interviewed, including those who had instituted the charges against CRS. The twenty-seven-page report, made public in November 1985, fully exonerated CRS of charges of misuse of funds.

The commission then drew attention to the fact that the situation in Ethiopia had at best "improved marginally" during the past year, and that nearly six million people were still at risk. The real danger, the report concluded, was "donor fatigue," a danger the commission hoped its finding would help avert.[23]

"As they looked to the immediate future, the partners saw little prospect of an early end to the Ethiopian emergency. Each month they discovered new areas of need."

"If the team concluded that the needs projected by the U.S. government were understated, its report would become the instrument the cooperating agencies could use to press for additional resources."

"At the October meeting the executives reaffirmed their determination to continue the joint CDAA/E program, especially in view of the uncertainty of the 1986 food allocation."

XI

Threat to Unity ─────────────

THE DISCUSSIONS concerning the payment of inland transport costs for the 1984–85 food grants had not been concluded when the time arrived to prepare requests for 1985–86. The next fiscal year of the U.S. government began on October 1, 1985, and at least four to six months could be expected to elapse between a grant application and the actual delivery of food in Ethiopia.

Washington had approved the CDAA/E request for 1984–85 in November 1984, but apart from a small shipment of grain diverted while en route to another destination, no CDAA/E food arrived in Ethiopia until February 21, 1985. Even by mid-June, when the new request was submitted to AID, only 40,000 tons of the 1984–85 request had reached Ethiopia. CDAA/E had been advised that by the end of the fiscal year on September 30, 1985, monthly allocations would bring the final total to only 161,000 of the requested 225,000 tons.[1]

As they looked to the immediate future, the partners saw little prospect of an early end to the Ethiopian emergency. Each month they discovered new areas of need. By June 1985, the number of operating centers had increased to more than ninety. More than 1,200 care-givers were at work. Even

in areas where early spring rains had given some encouragement, hopes dwindled as crops withered under returning
drought. As the planting season for major autumn harvests
approached, few farmers in the drought-stricken areas even
had seeds to plant.

Some success had been achieved in reducing the size of
the huge camps, but the camps themselves had by no means
been eradicated. One of the largest, at Ibenat in Gondar, became the subject of a worldwide scandal in late April 1985,
when local party officials, aided by army units, forcibly evac-
uated 36,000 famine victims and burned their grass huts in
an effort to return the peasants to the land. Kurt Jansson,
U.N relief coordinator, visited the scene personally, and with
the support of the RRC and the voluntary agencies, was able
to repair some of the damage and arrange for the restoration
of the camp.[2]

On the basis of documentation drawn from the first six
months of CDAA/E operation, CRS submitted a new request
to AID on June 17, 1985, for 226,000 tons of food. Although
the new fiscal year did not begin until October 1, John Donnelly, director of material resources and grants administration
for CRS in New York, asked for an implementation date of
July 1, 1985, with the expectation that if his proposal were
approved, the initial shipments could be in Ethiopia on October 1.

In his letter accompanying the operational plan, Donnelly
wrote, "Last January the CRS/CDAA was only a concept....
Six months later, the dream is a reality. A multi-faceted network now exists, with the capability to reach two million
recipients. As to the future, we recognize the uncertainties of
potential harvests, rains, and migrations.... We must prepare
for a 'worst case scenario' and thus seek the commitment
of AID to this twelve-month proposal. Should the rains be
sufficient and harvests produced in adequate quantities, then
the commitment can be scaled back. Forward planning dic-
tates that the luxury of month-to-month support cannot be
applied at this time."[3]

U.S. Scales Down Food Grants

The AID offices, however, were not prepared to accept Donnelly's rationale. Steven Singer, deputy director of Food for
Peace, acknowledged that longer lead times were inherent
in well-planned aid programs and indicated AID's willingness to make a "resource allocation" of 75,000 tons to assure a response to needs early in the new fiscal year. But
the situation in Ethiopia, he said, was "fluid." The needs
in 1986, for instance, would depend on the harvest at
the end of the year. A twelve-month commitment by AID
was impossible. Moreover, reflecting Peter McPherson's complaint over the Ethiopian government's failure to clear the
backlog in the ports of Assab and Massawa, he suggested
that the government's ability to accomplish that would be
a key indicator of its commitment to a continued relief
program.[4]

By August AID had decided not only to scale down the
size of the "resource allocation" for CDAA/E that Steven
Singer had thought reasonable in June; it had also decided
to reduce the total amount of food assistance to Ethiopia for
the coming year. Julia Chang Bloch stated AID's position in
a letter to Lawrence Pezzullo. "The rains," she wrote, "have
been good, and we are hopeful that this will translate into
substantially improved crop production." According to her
sources, conditions had improved to the extent that the estimated food deficit in Ethiopia in 1985–86 would be only
900,000 tons, instead of 1.3 million, as in 1984–85. Apply-
ing its policy of providing one-third of the total emergency
food requirement for Ethiopia, the U.S. government had supplied a total of 470,000 tons in 1984–85, of which CDAA/E
had received 161,000 tons. For 1985–86, still maintaining the
same policy, AID anticipated approving a total of 300,000
tons, of which the partnership could expect to receive about
100,000 tons.

Conflicting Assessments of Need

Other factors, too, Bloch explained, now had begun to play
a role. "We are now at that critical stage of our food assistance programs," she wrote, "where we must assure that
our food assistance does not create dependencies nor act as
a disincentive to agricultural production." In implementing
this policy, AID announced that all new requests from voluntary agencies for 1985–86 would be reduced by 50 percent.
CDAA/E was advised that it could anticipate a 1985–86 allocation of about 90,000 tons, less than 50 percent of the
agency's request. Instead of an initial "resource allocation" of
75,000 tons, AID now stated its intention to seek approval
for 35,000 tons, with the balance in quarterly allocations
throughout the fiscal year.[5]

The fact that the cuts were based upon the 1985–86 requests from the voluntary agencies, rather than upon the
programs established and conducted in 1984–85, appeared to
CRS to grant an unfair advantage to new and inexperienced
agencies and to discriminate against CDAA/E. William E.
Schaufele, former U.S. assistant secretary of state for African
affairs, who had replaced Kenneth Hackett as CRS senior director for Sub-Sahara Africa in May 1985, saw CDAA/E pay-
ing a penalty for having been on the spot at the right time in
1984. The CDAA/E partners, with assistance from AID, had
gone to great expense to establish the necessary organization
and structure to mount the largest private emergency feeding
operation ever undertaken. To require a massive and costly
dismantling of such a successful program, while encouraging
newer organizations to expand their operations, seemed both
uneconomic and discriminatory. Moreover, to make such a
decision before any systematic assessment of the continuing
needs of the people in Ethiopia or the prospects for the coming harvests had been made appeared to Schaufele to be
irresponsible.[6]

Coming as it did on the heels of the extended and often
bitter struggle over the payment of inland transport costs,
the controversy over the 1985–86 food allocations raised ten-

sions between CRS and AID to an acute level. CRS officials felt AID was encouraging other agencies to apply for food, not only for Ethiopia but elsewhere in the world, as if to counteract CRS domination of the PL-480 Title II food program. Harsh words were exchanged on several occasions, and when CRS came under attack in the public press during the summer of 1985, AID officials no doubt felt some empathy with CRS's accusers. One senior AID official cited the published correspondence relating to this controversy as an example of the distrust and hostility displayed by CRS toward AID, "its major partner in responding to the African famine."[7]

In any event, CRS, acting for the CDAA/E partnership, was not ready to accept AID's decisions on food allocation as final. Before initiating any counteraction, CRS felt that an independent needs assessment should be conducted in collaboration with ECS, EECMY, LWR, and LWF. The decision was made to call in a reputable consulting firm, which would be assisted by selected representatives from the cooperating agencies. The results of such a study would allow the cooperating sponsors to present their views, plan their programs, and determine the amount of resources needed for support. Using the most current data from the RRC and the U.N. Food and Agriculture Organization, it would evaluate conflicting current estimates of needs, including the Atwood Report, on which AID had based its reduction of food grants for 1985–86. The Atwood Report, commissioned by AID, had been issued in September 1985, before any data on the current harvest was available.

If the team concluded that the needs projected by the U.S. government were understated, its report would become the instrument the cooperating agencies could use to press both the U.S. and other governments for additional resources. Preparations were made for a team representing a firm called Intertect, Inc., to spend two to three weeks in Ethiopia in December 1985. Selected representatives of the cooperating agencies would be available to provide resource and information support to the consultants.[8]

138   THREAT TO UNITY

Tensions within the Partnership

Before the team could begin its assignment, however, a series
of internal developments caused the partners of CDAA/E
once again to reexamine their mutual relationships and the
nature of their partnership.

The problem of payment for internal transport persisted
throughout the summer of 1985. As late as June 26, there
was still no answer on how a $4.5 million deficit created by
AID's default would be paid. CRS agreed to cover $1.5 mil-
lion, but the other partners felt CRS should take responsibility for the entire amount since CRS had made the original
agreements with AID and had assured the partners that all
transport and administrative costs would be paid.

Moreover, the partners were also aware of the $50 mil-
lion fund accumulated by CRS from private donations, which
CRS had allocated for the support of its Omnibus Program.
Whatever portion of the inland transport deficit EECMY/
LWF, ECS, or any of the smaller distributing agencies would
pay would represent, they believed, an indirect and invol-
untary contribution by the partners to the CRS Omnibus
program.

The press controversy initiated by James MacGuire's allegations against CRS had also affected the CDAA/E, distract-
ing both leaders and staff and mounting a subtle assault on
the trust level among the partners. With the integrity of the
entire program called into question, it was impossible simply to ignore the charges. When the coordinators and even
the Executive Committee met, tensions rose over matters that
would ordinarily have been routinely handled.

The truck shortage continued to cause problems throughout the summer. The relief promised by bringing in haulers
from Kenya seemed plagued by delays. At one point in
August EECMY/LWF complained that the primary distribution point at Nazareth, which was supplied by CRS, was
out of grain, and the distributing agencies supervised by
EECMY/LWF were therefore unable to supply their centers.
CRS logistics countered with complaints that EECMY/LWF

was lax in submitting reports and had failed to offer their trucks to help transport food from the port of Assab to Nazareth.[9]

When, therefore, the all-consuming issue of the impending 50 percent slash of the 1985–86 food grant was broached in an Executive Committee meeting on August 16, the undercurrent of insecurity immediately broke into the open. Before responding to such a critical issue, the executives felt they ought to reexamine the future of the whole CDAA/E operation.

To take up these questions they scheduled a special meeting for the following week, on August 21. The meeting was postponed, rescheduled, and finally canceled. During the entire month of September, when a sharing of information and mutual counsel might have relieved some of the tensions and uncertainties felt by all the partners, no meetings of the Executive Committee were held.[10]

Finally, in early October, the executives gathered for a "brainstorming" session. Impatient with the extended controversy over inland transport costs and concerned that CRS intransigence might be a factor in AID's intended reduction of the 1985–86 food allocation to CDAA/E, Niels Nikolaisen, LWF resident representative, proposed an independent LWF request of 100,000 tons to AID, approximately one-half of the request submitted on behalf of the partnership by CRS.

Within the next few days and without further consultation with the Executive Committee, Nikolaisen requested and received approval from LWF in Geneva. Fred Fischer, USAID representative in Addis Ababa, indicated that his agency was open, even favorable, to such a request. It was Nikolaisen's hope that a separate request to AID would result in an increased total tonnage for the partnership, but he also saw it as an opportunity for EECMY/LWF to gain a greater degree of independence in the handling and distributing of food. He even expressed the readiness of LWF to pay 50 percent of the inland transport costs, a suggestion that was no doubt welcomed by USAID. Fischer, however, made it clear that a separate allocation to LWF would not increase the total grant of 90,000 tons to the partnership. Overall tonnage for Ethiopia would still remain at 300,000 tons.[11]

Francis Carlin first learned in conversation with the local USAID office that LWF had actually presented a request for a separate allocation. After registering surprise at Nikolaisen's unilateral move, he simply acknowledged LWF's right to do so. But in a telex to William Schaufele in New York, he recalled that the CDAA/E partnership was originally slated to close down at the end of 1985. Although the emergency in Ethiopia had not yet passed, he thought recent developments suggested that such a turn of events might actually be best for all concerned. He was sure that all CDAA/E members would still want to continue cooperation and joint planning to avoid duplication in their programs, but phasing out CDAA/E would solve the persistent problem of its uncertain status with the government of Ethiopia. It would ease the problem of CRS's high visibility, which had created such concern for ECS. It would also give LWF the greater degree of independence it apparently desired. Carlin concluded by indicating his support for such a move and his intention to call a meeting of the Executive Committee to solicit their reaction. In the meantime he asked for policy guidance from CRS in New York.[12]

After a telephone consultation with Norman Barth, at Lutheran World Relief, Schaufele's response to Carlin left no doubt that CRS/New York felt that the joint operation should be maintained. Separate applications from CRS and LWF would probably result in smaller allocations for all voluntary agencies, including both CRS and LWF. Instead of dividing efforts, he felt, this was the time for strong, coordinated pressure to influence the decision-making process in Washington.

Schaufele had also spoken with AID officials in Washington. They, too, supported the continuance of CDAA/E. He advised them, however, that if the proposed reductions in food ceilings and allocations were implemented, CRS, in the interest of good management and effective programming, would have to reassess its relationship with its partners. Very likely the infrastructure and the system of food distribution that had been so successfully organized would have to be dismantled.[13]

Decision for Unity

When the CDAA/E Executive Committee assembled on October 19 in Addis Ababa, Carlin reported Schaufele's message from CRS and LWR, strongly urging continued cooperation through CDAA/E. Not ready to accept instructions from New York, however, Nikolaisen responded that his Geneva headquarters had left the decision in his hands regarding submission of an independent request to USAID.

The committee felt that a separate proposal need not dissolve the partnership. In fact, it expressed the unanimous desire that "no matter what occurs, we will maintain the common program design and close working cooperation and coordination that now exists." Certain changes in the CDAA/E mechanism, however, might be necessary, and for a determination of appropriate actions the Executive Committee scheduled a full day working session on October 23. Both USAID in Addis Ababa and CRS in New York were advised of the committee's position.[14]

Before the full-day meeting, Executive Committee members met with Fred Fischer of USAID. Their purpose was to explain to Fischer that whether they submitted a single request or a divided request, they had no intention of dissolving the partnership, and that their total request for FY 1986 remained at 225,000 tons. Fischer reiterated his openness to either approach, but stated that until he received written notice of change from CDAA/E, the original single CDAA/E request would stand.

At the October 23 meeting the executives reaffirmed their determination to continue the joint CDAA/E program, especially in view of the uncertainty of the 1986 food allocation. They discussed the continued need for coordination of field operations and the maintenance of a small secretariat, and decided to move the CDAA/E offices out of the ECS building as soon as another appropriate location could be found. They also endorsed the formation of a joint assessment team from the partnership, proposed earlier by CRS as an adjunct to the Intertect assessment, to study and recommend program criteria and ration levels for 1986 and to prepare justifications for expanded 1986 levels of support.

Another highly significant action emerged from the October 23 meeting. As stated in the official message dispatched by the Executive Committee to their parent bodies in the United States and Europe, "All partners considered it important to form a joint team of Ethiopian church leaders from EECMY, ECS, and Ethiopian Orthodox Church, with the objective of going to the United States to press for continued and expanded support from the U.S. government."[15]

The response to this suggestion from the parent agencies in both the United States and Europe was enthusiastic. While a great deal of planning and preparation would be necessary in the ensuing weeks, the proposal would eventually come to fruition in March 1986. For the first time in their history the three Christian communities in Ethiopia would join together in a common mission. They would remind the world that there was still great need in their country, but they would also express appreciation to the people and governments of the United States, Canada, and Europe for their generous outreach to the people of Ethiopia.

An Act of Faith

When the assessment team endorsed by the Executive Committee on October 23 assembled in Addis in November, it was confronted by the greatly reduced food allocations that AID had recently made public. The CDAA/E allotment had been set at 90,000 tons, well below the 226,000 tons requested by CRS in June, and even further below the 252,000 tons CDAA/E food programmers now thought necessary to

meet current and continuing requirements of 21,000 tons per
month.

In a joint meeting on November 20, the CDAA/E Executive Committee and the visiting assessment team set forth a
strategy in a position paper on the 1986 joint famine relief
needs of ECS, EECMY, CRS, and LWF. The paper reaffirmed
the commitment of the partners to "maintaining where necessary the starving Ethiopian population from 1985 through
1986." It also acknowledged a "moral obligation to provide
wherever possible for additional needy victims as yet unas-
sisted" in different regions of the country.

If the CDAA/E allocation were to be limited to 90,000
tons for nine months in fiscal 1986, the current program
level would have to be reduced by 35.2 percent, or 7,000
tons per month. More than a half-million starving Ethiopians
each month would suddenly be deprived of life-sustaining
food. If the announced cut should actually be imposed, CRS
proposed calling forward the entire 1985–86 allocation of
U.S. government commodities early and maintaining a full
program as long as the food supply lasted, if only for six
months. Such an action would serve as a signal to the world
that the four church agencies were committed to provide the
necessary food support. It might also move the U.S. government and other donors to come through with more tonnages
later in the year.[16]

Following the recommendations of the assessment team,
the partners proposed to begin by calling forward immediately the first 75,000 tons of the AID commitment. According to their best estimates, at the end of 1985 there
would still be 20,000 tons, either in the pipeline or in
CDAA/E warehouses in Ethiopia. This supply would maintain the program until the new AID food began to arrive,
probably in March 1986. The European Economic Community had already agreed to ship 10,000 tons. A Swedish
government-supported airlift mediated by LWF, operating
since September 1985, was carrying nearly 2,000 tons of
food per month into Eritrea and Tigray. By calling forward
the remaining 15,000 tons of the AID allocation, the full pro-

gram of 21,000 tons per month could be maintained through June 1986.[17]

Beyond June 30, however, lay the prospect of a 132,000-ton shortfall and two million hungry and abandoned people. The CDAA/E partners had no further documented assurances from donors. Each of the partners was prepared to ask its parent agencies in New York and in Europe for a million dollars to purchase food on the open market, but the cash costs of purchasing and transporting the six-month shortfall would approximate $40 million. There would be additional appeals to the EEC, agencies related to Caritas and LWF, and governments in Europe, Australia, Canada, and the United States. But there were no commitments in sight and little prospect of any change in the allocation from AID.

*"AID's reduction of the 1986 food alloca-
tion could well have been a fatal blow to
CDAA/E. Instead, the action actually rejuvenated the partnership and launched it into 1986
with greater strength and enthusiasm than ever."*

*"A clear sign of the rejuvenated spirit in the
partnership was the Executive Committee's decision
to abandon the name Churches Drought Action
Africa/Ethiopia (CDAA/E). They agreed that they
would use the individual names of the agencies,
but that informally their cooperative efforts would
be referred to as the Joint Relief Partnership."*

*"Assured of the availability of U.S. food
and permission to use it right away, the JRP
partners were free to turn their full attention
to other potential donors to supply the program needs for the remaining months of 1986."*

XII

The Partnership Reaffirmed ——

As THE FIRST YEAR OF ITS OPERATION drew to a close in late October 1985, the partners of the CDAA in Ethiopia were genuinely discouraged. CRS had been fighting off press attacks all summer and jousting with the U.S. government over transport costs. The Krol Commission sent by the U.S. Catholic Bishops Conference had spent weeks probing its records. ECS was still pressing the partnership to move their offices out of its building. The RRC was impatient with all the partners because of their reluctance to sign operating agreements with the Ethiopian government. LWF's restlessness had been manifested in Niels Nikolaisen's request for a separate allocation from AID. Some members of the CDAA/E Executive Committee felt it was time to raise further questions about its future.

Under these circumstances the 50 percent reduction of the 1986 food allocation by AID could well have been a fatal blow to CDAA/E. Instead, AID's action actually rejuvenated the partnership and launched it into 1986 with greater strength and enthusiasm than ever.

There were several developments that contributed to this remarkable change. The response Francis Carlin had received from both Catholics and Lutherans in New York when he reported on Nikolaisen's proposal to USAID — a resounding expression of confidence in the effectiveness of a united front — was underscored by the visiting assessment team that met with the Executive Committee and key staff members to discuss plans for 1986. The position paper that formed the basis for their discussion emphasized words such as "commitment" and "belief." "Nothing can be more urgent," it declared, "than saving lives at risk. . . . People of all nations responded in 1985 to the largest relief effort of all time. We pray that they not fail those still starving in 1986."[1]

Consultations had also taken place between LWR in New York and LWF in Geneva, and following their counsel, Niels Nikolaisen finally agreed to withdraw his request for a separate allocation from AID. The prospects of a visit by Ethiopian church leaders to North America and Europe looked promising to both the partners in Ethiopia and their colleagues overseas.[2]

As the year ended, members of the partnership were also encouraged by the reports summarizing their accomplishments during their first year of operation. In addition to the substantial relief, rehabilitation, and service programs conducted independently by each of the partners, they had jointly, through the CDAA/E, distributed a total of 206,872 tons of cereals, milk powder, and vegetable oils, valued at $70 million. Most of the 1,825,295 persons who benefited from this food were family members or destitute persons who had received monthly take-home rations. Thousands of malnourished children had also received daily rations at more than a hundred feeding centers throughout the country.

All the food had been donated, mostly by governments. AID had provided to CDAA/E alone 161,194 tons, valued at $53,277,100, with $51,410,000 in addition, to cover the costs of transporting the food and operating the centers.[3] The remaining 45,678 tons valued at $17,756,235, and $5,992,955 for transport costs were provided by the governments of Sweden, Canada, Australia, and the European Economic Community.[4]

These and other governments had also donated additional thousands of tons of food and relief supplies directly to each of the partner agencies, to be used in their regular or special programs. According to a general agreement among the partners, only grants of 5,000 tons or more were ordinarily directed to the joint program. Smaller amounts were generally used within the individual agency programs.

JRP: A New Name for a New Day

A clear sign of the rejuvenated spirit in the partnership was the Executive Committee's decision to abandon the name Churches Drought Action Africa/Ethiopia. In November, they agreed that in official communications, they would use the individual names of the agencies, but that informally their cooperative efforts would be referred to as the Joint Relief Partnership (JRP).[5]

Since the original documents had been drawn up in the expectation of a one-year emergency, the beginning of a second year was an appropriate time for revision. A new version of the Statement of Intent was prepared, describing "the cooperation" between the partners as "The Joint Relief Programme of ECS/EECMY/CRS/LWF-Ethiopia." Corresponding changes were made in the contracts between CRS and its partners, and between each partner and the distributing agencies within their areas of supervision. Instead of the description of a secretariat and technical staff, a new Outline of Working Relationship identified the JRP Food and Nutrition Programming Coordinator as the single staff person responsible to the Executive Committee. Regular meetings of the Executive Committee and of the coordinators of each partner agency continued as before.[6]

As the streamlined version of the JRP began operation in its own office late in January 1986, it had a new chief officer, an Ethiopian woman, Sister Azeb Tekle. A professional nurse, Sister Azeb had served as project manager of a feeding center in Sidamo for Redd Barna (Norwegian Save the Children). In 1985, she had worked with the JRP as trainer and supervisor of the teams that operated the feeding program for the cooperating agencies. Sister Azeb was appointed by the Executive Committee as acting coordinator and nutrition programmer for the JRP in January 1986. She assumed full responsibility as coordinator in April.[7]

Checking in with the RRC

As the official relief arm of the Ethiopian government, the RRC maintained the prerogative of approving or excluding any foreign relief agency desiring to operate in Ethiopia. The partners of CDAA/E had never questioned this right, and their Statement of Aims and Objectives had declared their intention to conduct their relief activities in consultation with the RRC. The detailed description of the Famine Intervention Program and the Plan of Operation drawn up to support their request for emergency food from the U.S. government had been submitted to the RRC for its approval. Since the RRC was also the official distributing agency for food sent to Ethiopia through government-to-government grants, it was essential for CDAA/E to coordinate its more specialized supplementary nutrition intervention program with the much larger general distribution by the RRC.

Because of the proliferation of foreign groups and agencies entering Ethiopia when news of the famine broke, the RRC drew up a standard agreement, which it expected each agency to sign. Many agencies resisted the government's request. Maintaining that it was not an agency, the CDAA/E had claimed it could not sign a legal document. Both the ECS and EECMY claimed exemption as indigenous church institutions. CRS had signed a separate agreement in 1975, and was not eager to modify it.[8] LWF had no agreement, but was closely identified with the Mekane Yesus Church.

The two international agencies, LWF and CRS, continued to raise objections to specific items in the agreement that they felt limited their activities. Most objectionable to them was the requirement that when a project activity ended, any capital equipment such as vehicles would become the property of the government. Actually, there were probably more benefits than restrictions in the agreement, including the assurance of duty-free import of food and supplies, special arrangements for currency exchange, the use of vehicles, and above all the assurance that their operations in outlying villages and towns would be free from interference by local authorities or party functionaries.[9]

In the closing months of 1985 the patience of government officials began wearing thin, especially over the number of voluntary agencies and international staff being brought into the country. Although neither CRS nor LWF, with their strong indigenous connections, was cited in the RRC complaint, Commissioner Dawit noted a 75 percent increase in expatriate staff, from 318 to 556 persons, between January and June 1985. In contrast, at the end of 1985 CRS and LWF, the largest distributors of relief food among the voluntary agencies, each employed only fifteen and fourteen internationals, respectively, on their professional staffs.[10]

The RRC also indicated its intention to exercise stricter control over the voluntary agencies in authorizing areas of the country in which they might operate and in the approval of ration levels for agencies engaged in feeding programs. These concerns probably encouraged both LWF and CRS to overlook several minor objections to portions of the agreement and sign, though they were the last among the agencies to do so.[11]

On the issue of the continuing emergency in Ethiopia and the need for an unabated flow of food into the country, the RRC and the partners of the JRP were in full agreement. In his final appearance before a donors' meeting in Addis Ababa on October 8, 1985, Commissioner Dawit expressed his thanks to donor countries and especially to Kurt Jansson, who was completing his one-year assignment as United Nations assistant secretary general for emergency operations in Ethiopia. Dawit sounded a hopeful note, recognizing that great progress had been made during the course of the year, but urging continued assistance lest the fragile recovery be jeopardized.

Dawit's plea and the RRC assessment of needs for 1986 gave strong support to the JRP proposal to the U.S. government for a 226,000-ton grant for 1986, virtually equivalent to that requested for 1985. The RRC assessment, based on its highly-regarded Early Warning System, projected a shortfall of 1.2 million tons of emergency food in 1986, affecting 5.8 million people.[12] The Atwood Report, submitted to AID in September, before data on the current harvest was available, had projected a shortfall of only 911,000 tons for the Fiscal Year 1986.[13]

In a letter on January 3, 1986, to Ahmed Ali, head of aid coordination and international relations for the RRC, and signed by the four executives of the partner agencies, the JRP submitted its Joint Relief Plan for the first six months of 1986. In careful observance of RRC requirements, it detailed the number of monthly beneficiaries, the tonnages to be distributed regionally, and the supplementary monthly rations for each family. The executives expressed the hope that their program would be supportive of the general RRC plan for the country and affirmed their readiness to finalize their plans in a formal agreement. Explaining that the JRP currently had commitments sufficient to carry out their program for only six months, they anticipated submitting a second proposal when commitments were assured for July to December 1986. The JRP operational plan was approved by the RRC within weeks, and a formal agreement was signed by the four agency executives and the RRC Commissioner in April.[14]

Confrontation at the U.S. Embassy

Even as relations with the RRC improved, the tensions that had marred communications between CRS in New York and AID in Washington made themselves felt in the corresponding offices in Ethiopia. CRS suspected that the reduction in the JRP allocation for 1986, while some other agencies received increased allotments, was intended as a rebuke to CRS. The encouragement of the USAID office in Addis Ababa of Niels Nikolaisen's request for an independent LWF/LWR grant in October and November 1985 gave support to such a view.

On its part USAID saw the JRP proposal to utilize the full amount of the reduced 1986 grant in six months as a transparent move by CRS to pressure AID into making additional food available later in the year. The unusual alacrity with which the newly-renamed JRP sought the approval of the RRC for its six-month Plan of Operation conveyed the same impression.

When Francis Carlin, on behalf of JRP, submitted the same operational plan to USAID for its approval later in January, he received an angry response from Fred Fischer, USAID coordinator for emergency relief at the U.S. embassy in Addis Ababa, a copy of which was sent by telex to the State Department in Washington. Fischer complained that without consultation with USAID, the JRP had concluded an agreement with the RRC that would exhaust the total JRP allocation by July 1, three months before the end of the U.S. government's fiscal year. Until a revised operational plan, adjusted to the projected reduction of the AID grant, was submitted by the JRP, Fischer suspended any further "call forwards" or approvals within the 90,000-ton allocation to JRP. Such a revised plan, with more documentation, was to be submitted before the official program review scheduled at the U.S. embassy on February 7.[15]

At the embassy meeting in February the confrontation continued. Visiting AID staff from Washington were present. Each partner agency had been invited to bring additional persons from its relief team. William Schaufele, senior regional director for Sub-Sahara Africa, flew in from New York to represent CRS headquarters. In all, about twenty people were seated around a long table. For USAID, Fred Fischer reiterated the charges he had made in his letter and repeated the rationale for the reduced allocation of 90,000 tons. For the partners, Francis Carlin reminded Fischer that the original JRP Plan of Operation for 1986 requesting 226,000 tons had been presented to AID in Washington on June 17, 1985, and had not been withdrawn. Since then, the official relief agency of the Ethiopian government had confirmed its estimate of needs.

The USAID staff responded by asking how the JRP intended to carry out its proposed program after the food supply ran out in June. Carlin responded, "We don't know. But in the name of humanity, we cannot agree to 90,000 tons for twelve months. We can tell you this. We are men and women of deep faith, and we believe God will provide that food."[16]

The meeting ended without any satisfactory understanding on plans for 1986. A week later Carlin wrote again to Fischer, providing the additional information the USAID official had requested on the six-month program of JRP, but reaffirming the continued validity of the JRP plan of June 17.[17] Meanwhile, Fischer's telex had reached the State Department in Washington, and Schaufele had returned to CRS in New York with a report on the stormy session at the U.S. embassy in Addis Ababa.

A Solution for Inland Transport Costs

Pezzullo and McPherson met privately in Washington on February 14, to try to repair the strained relations between CRS and AID. They began their discussion with the two issues that had sparked the dissension: the 1986 food allocation and the inland transport question.

The AID position on emergency food for Ethiopia, which McPherson felt obliged to defend, had been based on AID's more optimistic assessment of the famine conditions in Ethiopia. Even more controversial than the U.S. government's decision to reduce the overall quantity in keeping with its optimistic estimates, however, was AID's plan for allocating the 300,000 tons among the Private Voluntary Organizations (PVOs). The allocation involved a disproportionate reduction of the JRP grant.

McPherson did not contest Pezzullo's claims that AID
had increased its grants to other agencies, while cutting
funds for the partnership. He simply said there was not
enough food at hand to change the allocations already committed to other agencies. He did promise to make an effort
to find additional quantities and even held out the prospect
of drawing against the 1987 Fiscal Year to supply the months
of October to December 1986.

On the matter of inland transport for 1986, AID held to
the policy requiring voluntary agencies to pay 50 percent of
the costs. McPherson conceded in principle that the voluntary agencies ought not to be expected to bear that burden,
but explained that AID simply did not have the funds to
meet all requests. Once again, as in 1985, a compromise
understanding was reached, whereby the JRP portion would
be reimbursed through a set of complex funding exchanges.
The JRP partners would finally be obligated for only about
$2 million of the total $9 million for the inland transport of
90,000 tons of food.[18]

These concessions, however, were not sufficient to set the
minds of the JRP partners in Ethiopia at ease. When contracts between the partners and their distributing agencies
came up for renewal in January 1986, after the first year
of operation, the implementing agencies were advised that
because donor support had been reduced, the JRP would
no longer be able to cover the full costs of transporting
food from the primary warehouses to the operating sites.
Effective with the signing of the 1986 agreements, the agencies would be required to absorb these costs. A deadline of
March 1 was established after which, if the contracts were
not signed, no food would be delivered to the implementing
agency.

The agencies were assured that efforts would continue to
seek full funding from the U.S. government. CRS and LWF
agreed to pick up the costs for centers operated by the Catholic and Lutheran churches, but eight smaller distributing
agencies were faced with the possibility of closing their centers and withdrawing from the program. One of these, Irish

Concern, was obliged to terminate a program serving 6,000 families.[19]

As this issue was being worked through, the implementing agencies were first asked to pay $70 per ton, 50 percent of the transport costs from primary distribution points to the operating centers. The JRP partners agreed to absorb the rest. A welcome solution to the entire transport problem was finally reached in April 1986, when the U.S. government agreed to assume the full obligation for the inland transport of emergency food from shipboard to final distribution center.[20]

Pezzullo and McPherson concluded their meeting on February 14 with the understanding that key members of their respective staffs would be called together as soon as possible to confirm the agreements they had reached. To assure full representation, both Francis Carlin and Fred Fischer were brought in from Ethiopia by their respective agencies. William Schaufele of CRS and Richard Gold, Food for Peace officer with AID in Washington, headed the U.S.-based staffs. Meetings were held at CRS headquarters in New York. The central question was the same one that had been raised by the USAID staff in Addis: In view of the reduced grant from AID for 1986, how did the JRP expect to mount a program of 252,000 tons of food over a twelve-month period?

The CRS representatives brought to the meeting a revised operational plan for 1986 to replace the plan they had submitted to AID on June 17, 1985. Estimating two million beneficiaries and requesting 257,872 tons, the new plan actually projected a larger operation than in 1985. As of March 15, 1986, JRP reported, it had received assurances of 137,800 tons of food.

AID responded with a request that JRP supply a monthly projection for the distribution of 137,800 tons of food from January through September. Upon receipt of this projection AID declared its readiness to release immediately the balance of the 90,000 tons allocated to JRP.[21]

Thus assured of the availability of U.S. food and permission to use it right away, the JRP partners were free to turn their full attention to other potential donors to supply the program needs for the remaining months of 1986. They set high hopes on the anticipated personal visit of a team of Ethiopian church leaders to the donor countries of North America and Europe.

"The idea of a personalized food mission to North America first emerged in October 1985.... At the invitation of the ECS and EECMY, representatives of the three historic Christian communities gathered for a preliminary discussion of the proposed trip."

"They saw their journey as an opportunity to express the thanks of the people of Ethiopia for the life-sustaining gifts sent by the people of each nation they would visit. No one, however, attributed to the mission the enormous ecumenical significance that it was later seen to have had."

"Not long after their return, the three Ethiopian churches hosted a dinner for the ambassadors of the countries they had visited.... Members of the ecumenical team expressed satisfaction that their trip had helped to clear the confusion abroad concerning the persisting needs in Ethiopia.... But the historic achievement of the ecumenical journey was the opening of the doors of communication and friendship between the three great Christian communities within Ethiopia."

XIII

Ecumenical Journey ─────────

CONDITIONS HAD IMPROVED since the grim October of 1984 when hundreds were dying each week at Bati and Makelle. The camps had been emptied and death tolls were lower by far. But areas of severe need still existed in the country, as the Ethiopian government's Early Warning System clearly testified. In the face of international "donor fatigue," the RRC urged continued aid in 1986, but got little response. Governments were eager to withdraw. The United States led the way by reducing its food allocation 50 percent. AID officials spoke of terminating all emergency aid at the end of 1986.

The idea of a personalized food mission to North America first emerged in October 1985, in conversations between Francis Carlin and Kevin Delany, CRS information officer in Addis Ababa. At first they thought primarily of an appeal to the government and people of the United States by leaders of the Catholic and Lutheran churches of Ethiopia. In view of the unfriendly relations between the American and Ethiopian governments, they feared that the presence in the delegation of representatives of the Ethiopian Orthodox Church might actually hinder an appeal to the U.S. government for more aid. At the same time they realized that an appeal to the American public would be weakened if the EECMY and the ECS should presume to speak on behalf of the entire Christian community of Ethiopia. Questions would surely be raised about the absence of representation from the twenty-million-member Orthodox Church.

Leaders of the partnership, always sensitive to the local political and cultural climate, realized that ignoring the EOC might prevent the trip from taking place at all.[1] Official permission of the Ethiopian government would be needed for such international travel, and inevitably the question would be raised as to why the Orthodox Church, the national church of Ethiopia, was not included. Visas might be denied, or other obstructions placed in the way of their travel.

An even more delicate question was the compatibility of the church representatives. Lutherans and Catholics, already closely associated in the partnership, could travel together in harmony. But each of them had inherited a long history of mistrust, conflict, and even persecution by the Orthodox Church. A persisting residue of suspicion had been a major factor in the reluctance of both churches to invite the EOC to join the original consortium in 1984.

All the Ethiopian Christian churches had suffered at the hands of the Marxist government of Lt. Col. Mengistu. Following the Revolution in 1974, many church buildings, especially those of the EECMY, had been closed, pastors imprisoned, property confiscated. Monastery lands from which thousands of Orthodox monks gained their living had been seized, rendering the monks destitute. But the EOC remained the largest church, with historical ties to the state, and the other churches feared that government observers might have been sifted into its administrative ranks.

A History-Making Meeting

Nonetheless, "It was an historic meeting," recalled Kevin Delany, "the first time in many centuries they had ever sat down at a table together. You could have cut the air with the tension. There were a lot of formalities, and everyone was very stiff."[2]

Delany explained to the Ethiopians that he was present simply as a facilitator, and briefly indicated his understanding of the purpose of the proposed trip. All agreed that the objectives were, first, to ask the American people and people of other countries that might be added to the itinerary for more food assistance in 1986, and, second, to ask for more development aid in the coming years.

A third purpose emerged in subsequent sessions, as they began to look beyond the immediate needs of their people to the broader significance of their mission. As members of a team of church leaders, they saw their journey as an opportunity to express the thanks of the people of Ethiopia for the life-sustaining gifts sent by the people of each nation they would visit. No one, however, either among the delegation or among their JRP sponsors, attributed to the mission the enormous ecumenical significance that it was later seen to have had.

At the moment, practical concerns headed the agenda. Members of the group at first favored mid-January as an appropriate time for the trip, coinciding as it did with the return of Congress from its Christmas recess. It would be important, they thought, to seek appointments with highly ranked people in the administration and the Congress, and to involve the leaders of their counterpart churches in the United States in the appeal. No opportunity should be lost to inform the American people of the severe shortfalls of food anticipated for 1986.

The question arose concerning the allocation of additional food that might result from the trip. The JRP intended that any additional tonnage should be applied to the anticipated deficit in the total program during the second six months of 1986, after the current shipments from AID and EEC had been distributed. The EOC took the position that all food acquired through the appeal should be equally divided among the partners to use as each saw fit.[3]

Nine Distinguished Envoys

The question of membership on the ecumenical team evolved slowly during the weeks following the first meeting. It was agreed that there be nine members, three from each church. Each of the churches felt it important to include high-ranking church officials and persons directly involved in the famine intervention program. When final decisions were reached, nine leaders with impressive academic and professional credentials and wide international experience were ready to represent their country and their churches.[4]

Cardinal Paulos Tzadua, metropolitan archbishop of Addis Ababa, headed the Catholic delegates. Elevated to the College of Cardinals in 1985, Archbishop Paulos, a native of Eritrea, received his seminary training in his home province and held earned doctorates in both political science and law from the Catholic University of Milan in Italy. A recognized legal scholar and translator, he was fluent in seven languages, Italian, English, French, and Latin, as well as three Ethiopian languages: Amharic, Tigrigna, and the ancient ecclesiastical language, Ge'ez.

The second member of the Catholic team was Father Kidane Mariam Ghebray, secretary general of the Ethiopian Catholic Secretariat since August 1985 and a priest of the eparchy of Adigrat in Tigray province, where he had also served as director of studies and rector of the theological seminary. He had studied at the Pontifical Urban University in Rome for eight years, earning licentiates in theology and philosophy. Cambridge University in England had awarded him a certificate in English proficiency and after a year of further study in Magdalen College, a postgraduate certificate in education.

Sister Maura O'Donahue was the only non-Ethiopian among the delegates. A medical doctor of the Medical Missionaries of Mary, Sister Maura was born in Ireland and received her medical training at University College, Dublin. In twenty-eight years of medical practice she had served in Nigeria, Spain, and Scotland, and, since 1974, in Ethiopia.

During the famine of 1984–85 she was medical consultant to the ECS in Addis Ababa.

The delegation from the Ethiopian Evangelical Church Mekane Yesus was led by its lay president, Francis Stephanos. Ato*Francis earned a diploma and a certificate in Linguistics from the Ethiopian Evangelical College in Debre-Zeit and a certificate from the Gurakul Seminary. A teacher by profession, Ato Francis was vice-president of the Mekane Yesus Church for five years before his election as president in 1985. He was known as a strong advocate of ecumenical outreach.

Dr. Solomon Gidada, director of development of the Mekane Yesus Church, was one of the founders of the CDAA/E in 1984 and served as first chairman of its Executive Committee. A teacher and educational administrator by profession, Dr. Solomon received his higher education in the United States. He received B.S. and M.Ed. degrees from the University of Rochester and a doctorate in educational administration from Syracuse University. His intimate knowledge of the work of the JRP and his consistent support of its goals made him one of the most convincing spokespersons for the ecumenical mission.

The third delegate from the EECMY was Admasu Simeso, coordinator of relief efforts for the EECMY and for the Lutheran World Federation. Ato Admasu had also been a teacher before joining the famine relief staff in 1983. Educated in the United States, he earned a master's degree in International Relations from Wichita State University in Kansas.

Leading the delegation of the Ethiopian Orthodox Church was Dr. Abune Garima, archbishop of the EOC to the Sudan and executive secretary of the Development and Inter-Church Aid Department. Archbishop Garima, one of the fourteen bishops of the Holy Synod, had studied at church schools in Ethiopia and began his church career as a radio producer for the Ethiopian Orthodox Mission. Later he

---

*"Ato" is the Ethiopian equivalent of "Mr."

studied in Romania and earned a doctorate in theology. He
served as a priest in the Holy Trinity Cathedral in Addis
Ababa before being ordained bishop and then archbishop.

Abebaw Yegzaw, the second member of the Orthodox
team, was the general secretary of the Ethiopian Orthodox
Church. Like the archbishop, he had also begun his career
as a radio producer for the Ethiopian Orthodox Mission and
later became director of the mission and head of its Evangelical Department. He also studied in Romania and earned a
master's degree in theology. For several years before becoming general secretary of the church, he held various positions
in the Ethiopian government, including that of administrative
officer for the province of Gondar.

Completing the Orthodox delegation was Zemedhun Be-
zuwork, deputy executive secretary of the Development and
Inter-Church Aid Department of the EOC. Educated in the
United Kingdom in mass communications, Ato Zemedhun
had served his church in that field and, most recently, as
program director for DICAD.

While the churches were selecting their delegates, the
itinerary began to take shape. Offices of the World Council of
Churches and the Lutheran World Federation in Geneva encouraged inclusion of the European countries that had given
food support to the JRP. Canada had been added to the proposed itinerary almost immediately and was followed shortly
by the European capitals: Brussels (the headquarters of the
EEC), Stockholm, Bonn, Geneva, and Rome. Because of various schedule conflicts, the departure date was postponed to
March 7. Six days were set aside for New York and Washington, with the balance of the eighteen-day mission devoted
to the Canadian and European visits. The return to Addis
Ababa was scheduled for March 25.[5]

Preparing to Go

One of the concerns of the Americans who were involved
in preparations for the ecumenical journey was the kind of

reception the team might expect from the media. Delany advised the Ethiopians of both the hazards and opportunities they would encounter. He offered to compile a list of difficult questions that might be posed to them by reporters attempting to involve them in political issues. Before they left Addis Ababa, Delany conducted simulated press conferences and videotaped interviews to prepare members of the team, using actual questions they were most likely to be asked.

Echoes were still being heard from the press attacks on CRS, led by the *New York Times*. Reports of abuses inflicted by the Ethiopian government on its own citizens in implementing its resettlement program were appearing in American newspapers and periodicals. A group of French doctors, called Médecins sans Frontières, had been expelled by the Ethiopian government in December 1985 for exposing the forced resettlement of 600,000 farmers from the drought-ridden highlands in Wollo and Gondar to more productive lands in the west and south. Articles based upon their often exaggerated reports, such as the *Wall Street Journal* story of January 27, 1986, entitled "Today's Holocaust," gave full credence to the reports, concluding that the entire famine relief effort had served only to free up the resources of the Marxist government to carry out its military and political goals.

Members of the team were forewarned that they would be confronted with questions relating to resettlement and to "villagization," the Ethiopian version of collectivized farming, and to the status of the civil war in the northern provinces. In addition to these highly charged political questions, they could expect to be asked about the famine. Was the famine still severe? Was the food sent to Ethiopia reaching the people for whom it was intended? Was additional help really needed? More than a year had passed since the shock of starvation scenes on television screens had electrified the world. Now the government of the United States had reduced its allocations of food. Why should the flow of aid continue?[6]

Thanks to Seven Countries

Instead of assembling as a group at the Bole International
Airport in Addis Ababa for a festive joint departure on
March 7, two of the Mekane Yesus representatives had already left for New York several days earlier. Cardinal Paulos
had gone ahead to Rome. Kevin Delany remembered that as
they waited for their flight to be called, each group stood in
a separate cluster surrounded by its own well-wishers. There
was TV coverage. Commissioner Dawit was on hand to express the good wishes of the government. But there was no
sign of special conviviality.[7]

The United States

The group arrived in New York on Saturday afternoon,
March 8. After a Sunday of rest and worship in churches of
their respective communions, they began a two-day schedule of visits. At the request of the Orthodox delegation, they
called first on the Ethiopian ambassador to the United Nations, Berhanu Dinka, and their first press conference, mod-
erated by Kevin Delany, took place at the Church Center
at the United Nations. The group had agreed that at each
appearance they would address three themes: first, the appreciation of the Ethiopian people for the assistance given
by the people and government of the United States; second,
the famine condition in Ethiopia during the past eighteen
months; and, third, the food outlook in 1986. Spokespersons
for each church would alternate in making these statements;
questions could be answered by any of the delegates.[8]

Interviews continued after a luncheon hosted by Cardinal
John O'Connor, archbishop of New York, at the headquarters
of the Catholic Relief Services. Speaking as the head of the
Catholic delegation, Cardinal Paulos expressed thanks "to
the institutions, churches, and individuals who undertook
sacrifices to help our needy people." Orthodox Archbishop
Garima assured the American people that the memory of the

1985 assistance "will remain in the hearts and minds of several generations as a generous human act." President Francis Stephanos sounded a note of urgency concerning the continuing crisis. "With so many lives hanging in the balance," he said, "we can't afford to relax until we have the grain in our hands. That is why we are visiting the seven countries."[9]

Major events of the second day in New York included a visit with the secretary general of the United Nations, Javier Pérez de Cuellar, and an ecumenical prayer service at the United Nations Church Center. Members of the Ethiopian delegation were joined by clergy and laity of American churches in petitions for the poor and needy in Ethiopia, in thanks for past assistance, and in prayer for peace, for future assistance, and for an end to the famine. Lutheran World Relief and Church World Service hosted a luncheon for the Ethiopian visitors at the Interchurch Center on Riverside Drive before they departed for Washington, D.C.

In Washington, the visitors joined in an ecumenical mass at St. Matthew's Cathedral and met with representatives of the Washington community of private voluntary agencies. But their main purpose in Washington was to present their case to key senators and representatives and to administrators of AID and the State Department. Efforts to secure appointments with the president of the United States and the secretary of state were not successful, even though it was made clear that these nine visitors were not political representatives of the Ethiopian government, but leaders of the three major Christian communities of Ethiopia.

Senator John Melcher of Montana and Congressman Ted Weiss of New York hosted receptions at the Capitol. In a brief meeting Chester Crocker, the assistant secretary of state for African affairs, told the visitors that the United States was doing all it could for Ethiopia and added that assistance would be easier if the Ethiopian government itself were more cooperative. In the absence of Peter McPherson, administrator of AID, the delegates were greeted by deputy AID administrator Jay Morris and came away from their contacts with these agencies with a feeling of having been treated in an unnecessarily brusque fashion and having been lectured rather than courteously listened to.

Canada

The Canadian visit on March 14 and 15 was divided between Ottawa and Montreal. The delegation was warmly welcomed by David MacDonald, coordinator for famine relief in the Department of External Affairs in Ottawa, and by Margaret Catley-Carlson, president of the Canadian International Development Agency (CIDA). MacDonald acknowledged the danger of "donor fatigue" and thanked the Ethiopians for reminding Canadians that millions in Ethiopia were still at risk. Catley-Carlson expressed strong interest in the long-term solution to the Ethiopian famine problem and assured the delegates of Canada's willingness to offer assistance.

Church agencies arranged ecumenical church services and receptions for the delegates. As in the United States, the media expressed concern over the Ethiopian government's controversial resettlement policy and asked about the attitude of the churches. Delegates responded that while the churches were not consulted or directly involved, they did not condone the abuses attributed to the government's program. They were, however, ready to assist any persons in need, regardless of religious or ethnic identities, including persons moved to new locations under the resettlement program. It would be unfortunate, however, Dr. Solomon stated, if world attention were focused only on the 600,000 involved in the resettlement while the six million in serious need were neglected.[10]

Europe

The first stop in Europe was Brussels, the headquarters of the EEC, which had contributed food to the JRP in 1985 and was being asked for more in 1986. Acting through member governments, the EEC was the second largest contributor of emergency food to Ethiopia, exceeded only by the United States. In 1985 it had provided 123,633 tons directly to the Ethiopian government and 49,511 additional tons to voluntary agencies. Of this 15,000 tons had been channeled through the JRP. For 1986 the JRP hoped to secure at least 20,000 tons.

Members of the ecumenical team arrived in Brussels on Sunday afternoon, March 15, and were received by representatives of Caritas/Belgium, Cardinal Godfried Daneells, and other church leaders. They also met with officials of the EEC, and with Leo Tindemans, Belgian minister of foreign affairs, who was also a member of the Council of Ministers of the European Community. Both he and Lorenzo Natali, vice-president of the EEC, acknowledged that the Ethiopian problem was not yet solved. They affirmed the Commission's readiness to provide additional assistance, both through government channels and through voluntary organizations.

In Sweden, the team was welcomed by representatives of the Lutheran Church and by the Ethiopian ambassador. Carl Tamm, director of the Swedish International Development Agency (SIDA) and Lena Wallen, minister of cooperation for international development, both assured the delegation of their continued support for long-range programs of development and agricultural improvement.

In the Federal Republic of Germany the visitors were warmly received by representatives of Caritas/Germany and leaders of the Protestant churches. Juergen Warnke, minister for international development and cooperation, reported that his government had earmarked 30,000 tons for voluntary agencies and that he would assure the JRP of an additional 15,000 tons. He also promised to support the JRP request to the EEC.[11]

The visit to Geneva gave opportunity to meet the leaders of the Lutheran World Federation and the World Council of Churches and to reflect more directly on the ecumenical di-

mensions of the journey. Dr. Emilio Castro, general secretary
of the WCC, invited members of the delegation to comment
on the effects of their travel together. Francis Stephanos re-
marked especially on the bridging of the separation all members had felt when the journey began. "At first," he recalled,
"when we moved into the airplane, everybody was sensitive
and sitting very quiet. But the more we stayed together, the
longer distance we traveled together, the more we needed to
talk together and play together. Some were sleeping, some
were laughing, some were walking, some were disappointed.
So we tried to understand one another. It was not only a
nice diplomatic relationship, but you saw somebody tired,
somebody weak, somebody exhausted, somebody laughing,
somebody hungry — all sorts of things. So we learned to
know each other."[12]

The final stop was Rome, for many of the delegates the
climax of their ecumenical journey. Members of Caritas Internationalis, the Catholic agency that had coordinated so
much support for Ethiopia through its network of member
societies throughout the world, members of Caritas Italiana,
and representatives of the Vatican itself welcomed the nine
travelers. Foreign Minister Giulio Andreotti assured them of
the Italian government's continued support. Crowning the
visit was a personal audience with His Holiness Pope John
Paul II. On Tuesday, March 25, the group returned to Addis
Ababa.[13]

"Why Can't We Walk Together?"

Not long after their return, the three Ethiopian churches
hosted a dinner for the ambassadors of the countries they
had visited to express their appreciation for the cordial reception extended to them by government officials and leaders of churches and voluntary agencies. In a written report
circulated at the dinner, members of the ecumenical team
expressed satisfaction that their trip had helped to clear the
confusion abroad concerning the persisting needs in Ethio-

pia. They rejoiced that in pursuing the common objective of serving the needy of their country, members of the delegation had been brought closer together.

As messages began to come in from governments and agencies, it became clear that their mission had also achieved its material purpose. Some members of the team had expressed disappointment that aid officials did not give specific responses at the time of their visits. Only in the Federal Republic of Germany had such an immediate commitment of 10,000 tons been made. But within days after their return to Ethiopia, the European Economic Community came through with a pledge of 20,000 tons, Sweden 6,000 tons, the Netherlands 2,000 tons, Australia 5,000 tons, and Italy 10,000 tons — a total of 53,000 tons. No additional commitments came from the United States or Canada, the initial targets of the proposed appeal, but extending the itinerary to include Europe had paid off. When added to the 120,000 tons already committed, the food pledged after the team's visit secured the JRP program through September 1986. Other requests were still pending, and with the U.S. government's new fiscal year beginning October 1, 1986, there was also some prospect of securing allocations for October through December under the FY-1987 emergency program.[14]

But the historic achievement of the ecumenical journey was the opening of the doors of communication and friendship between the three great Christian communities within Ethiopia. Years, even centuries, of mutual alienation and mistrust began to crumble as these leaders traveled and spoke together on behalf of all their hungry brothers and sisters. Francis Stephanos asked the key questions: "If we were able to travel together, why can't we work together? Why can't we walk together?"[15]

The first crucial steps had been taken. The next step was to take the Ethiopian Orthodox Church into the partnership. An invitation was extended to the EOC by the Executive Committee of the JRP to discuss ways and means. During the summer of 1986 a formal invitation was sent. Upon approval of the bishops of the Holy Synod, the Development and Inter-Church Aid Department of the EOC became a full member of the Joint Relief Partnership on March 3, 1987.[16]

"In May 1986, the JRP commissioned a long-range assessment of agricultural conditions and available food resources in Ethiopia....The recommendation led the JRP to continue programming emergency commodities during the remainder of 1986."

"Several features of the JRP venture gave it a distinctive character. Theirs was the largest of the private relief operations in Ethiopia and may have been the largest private famine relief venture ever undertaken."

"The crowning achievement of the JRP has been the realization of what many have called the 'Ecumenical Miracle,' ...the integration of the Roman Catholic and Lutheran relief networks...but also the instrument to break down walls that for fifteen hundred years had separated the Ethiopian Orthodox Church from most other members of the Christian community."

XIV

A Continuing Task ─────────

HAVING BEEN AMONG THE EARLIEST to identify the impending famine in 1982 and 1983, members of the JRP were more sensitive than most others to the dangers that could arise if relief agencies were to withdraw too rapidly. The fragile signs of recovery visible in early 1986 could be wiped out in a few weeks of extended drought or a visitation of locusts or army worms. Moreover, many farmers in the drought-devastated countryside still lacked seed and tools to plant crops or oxen to cultivate their fields. The extended food distribution network of the JRP that covered most of the country was also a sensitive system for detecting newly developing pockets of need.

As Francis Carlin reminded Fred Fischer in a letter written in April 1986, the closing down of International Red Cross Committee (ICRC) centers in Eritrea on the grounds of improved conditions had led at once to the inundation of ECS centers by needy people formerly served by ICRC.[1] Archbishop Thomas White, papal pro-nuncio in Addis Ababa, commended a policy of "famine recurrence prevention" to USAID and other major donors for what he called a "post-emergency" period. While some reduction in the numbers of outsiders in the famine relief "establishment" could be desirable, White observed, the machinery that had been so painstakingly put in place during the past eighteen

months ought not be completely dismantled before it was
certain that it would not be needed to meet another emergency in 1987 or 1988.[2]

Members of the ecumenical team who had urged international donors to continue their assistance based their plea
on realistic assessments by the RRC. JRP field observers, too,
keeping abreast of crop reports and harvest predictions in all
parts of the country, knew that while conditions improved
in Wollo and Shoa, lack of rain was producing severe food
shortages in Wollega and Ilubabor in the West and Hararge
in the South.

In May 1986, the JRP commissioned a long-range assessment of agricultural conditions and available food resources
in Ethiopia to help the partner agencies decide whether to
begin a phase-down of the JRP program. The recommendation of the team's forty-one-page report led the JRP to
continue programming emergency commodities at a level of
20,600 tons per month during the remainder of 1986. The
report warned that any decision to close down the relief
program entirely, even in 1987, should be approached with
extreme caution. "The situation remains far too unstable and
unpredictable," it concluded. "The risks are far too great to
err on the short side and cut food supplies prematurely."[3]

The wisdom of the decision to maintain the JRP structure
and program was underscored all too soon. In the southern province of Hararge, where food shortages compelled
the JRP virtually to double its feeding program in 1986, the
spring rains of 1987 failed completely. In late summer, the
major rains failed again in the northern highlands. By August
1987, the world learned that Ethiopia was in the throes of a
new crisis, affecting almost as many people as in 1984–85.

This time, however, some things were different. The
sprawling camps of Makelle, Bati, Korem, and Ibenat, to
which thousands of starving peasants had streamed in search
of food — or to die — were not recreated. The network of
distribution centers pioneered by the member agencies of the
JRP in 1984, to which drought victims could come to receive
life-sustaining rations for their families at home, was already

in place. The largest private famine intervention system in Ethiopia, with its logistic support network and its teams of trained staff at each distribution center, was the gift of the JRP to the Ethiopian people.

Legacy of the JRP

As early as July 1986, the Executive Committee of the JRP, conscious that they had carried through an unprecedented ecumenical venture in dealing with a major human crisis, took steps to document their experience. Realizing that it is not ordinarily in the nature of relief agencies to pause for extended reflection but rather to move from one existential crisis to the next, the JRP executives decided that a record of their experiences might be instructive for themselves and for others. They chose not only to assemble and make available the documentary records of their common enterprise, but to gather personal reflections through a series of recorded interviews. More than fifty persons who had been directly or indirectly involved in the work of the partnership shared their recollections of the operation itself and their assessments of its strengths and weaknesses.

Several features of the JRP venture gave it a distinctive character. Theirs was the largest of the private relief operations in Ethiopia during the famine of 1984–1986, and may have been the largest private famine relief venture ever undertaken. According to RRC estimates, between six and eight million people suffered from the famine. No one knows how many persons died. But the Nutrition Intervention Program of the JRP provided food rations for more than two million of these six to eight million victims through over one hundred distribution centers throughout the country. Over a two-year period, the JRP distributed a total of 428,000 tons of food.

The JRP itself was solely an emergency food program. Each of the member agencies, CRS, LWF, ECS, and EECMY, also conducted its own extensive programs of rehabilitation

and development; their cooperative venture through the JRP
was limited to distribution of emergency food. Nutrition and
health professionals carefully monitored the JRP programs.
This not only assured maximum benefits to recipients of
food, but made certain that the food was properly handled.

Considering the millions of people who were served, it is
even more remarkable that the personal, humane dimension
was not lost. The focus was on individual families, particularly on mothers and small children. People were dealt with
by name, and records of each child's growth were maintained. Mothers received counsel and instruction that would
benefit them and their families long after the famine emergency was over.

Hundreds of men and women received training as members of the teams that operated the centers. Skills they acquired were of lasting benefit to them personally and to
the families and communities of which they would later be
members.

The great strength of the partnership lay in the character
of its membership. Both the Ethiopian Catholic Church and
the EECMY were indigenous churches, deeply rooted in the
communities and culture of their country. Each church had
an established network of parishes, institutions, and trained
personnel that became the infrastructure for the JRP system
of food distribution. Other voluntary agencies had to bring
in personnel from abroad, establish new programs and operating centers, and always face the possibility of being asked
by the government to leave the country.

While both CRS and LWF, the foreign-based members
of the JRP, were not exempt from such a hazard, both had
been active in assisting their Ethiopian counterparts for many
years and were thus well-known to the Ethiopian government. Their presence assured powerful international support
and access to specialized technical expertise and to major
sources of food supply.

One of the truly remarkable features of the JRP was its
success in maintaining a major relief program in Ethiopia in
an extraordinarily sensitive political and military context. The

centerpiece of the JRP emergency program was the food and financial support given by the U.S. government. Yet one of the JRP members, CRS, had to lobby almost constantly from 1983 to 1986 to maintain support for the program, in the face of administration reluctance to give support to a country under a Marxist government.

EOC Becomes a Partner

The crowning achievement of the JRP has been the realization of what many have called the "Ecumenical Miracle." The integration of the Roman Catholic and Lutheran relief networks through Caritas Internationalis and CRS and the Lutheran World Federation has in itself been a witness to the way in which human need can draw individuals and churches together in common missions of mercy. But the JRP also became the instrument to break down walls that for fifteen hundred years had separated the Ethiopian Orthodox Church from most other members of the Christian community.

The full participation of the EOC in the JRP — expressing a common commitment to Christ's mandate to feed the hungry — has continued beyond the crisis that brought the churches together. As he returned from the ecumenical journey in March 1986, Archbishop Garima of the Ethiopian Orthodox Church expressed thanks to God on behalf of all the partners "that during the sufferings of millions of people we were able, irrespective of denominations, to think and act as Christians in the service of the needy people of Ethiopia."[4]

Appendix

Profile of JRP ————————————————

TERMS OF COOPERATION
FOR THE JOINT RELIEF PARTNERSHIP
OF ECS/EECMY/EOC/CRS/LWF
ETHIOPIA

AIMS, OBJECTIVES AND OUTLINE OF WORKING
RELATIONSHIP

AIMS AND OBJECTIVES

1. The Joint Relief Partnership of ECS, EECMY, EOC, CRS, LWF (hereinafter referred to as JRP) is not another voluntary agency, but the name adopted for an ecumenical effort set up by the Ethiopian Catholic Secretariat (ECS), the Ethiopian Evangelical Church Mekane Yesus (EECMY), Ethiopian Orthodox Church (EOC), the Catholic Relief Service (CRS), and the Lutheran World Federation (LWF) to coordinate a clearly-defined Famine Intervention Programme. The objectives of the JRP are:

    (a) to improve worldwide awareness of the nature and gravity of the famine crises facing the people of Ethiopia,

181

(b) to increase and pool resources for famine relief offered through the NGO sector to supplement bilateral and multilateral aid being given to the government of Ethiopia, and

(c) within the constraints of available resources, to support and expand existing NGO famine relief programmes and in consultation with the Relief and Rehabilitation Commission (RRC) of the Government of Ethiopia, encourage the identification of new programmes which will ensure the most effective distribution and utilization of available food aid.

OUTLINE OF WORKING RELATIONSHIP

2. The members of the JRP will maintain their own identity and continue their own regular programmes. At the same time they will come together to plan a Joint Famine Intervention Programme which will be implemented independently by each agency as well as other implementing agencies which a partner may sponsor in its designated region. The objectives are to acquire the donation of food supplies, and adequate funds to cover port clearance, inland transportation and distribution.

3. The policy decision-making body of the JRP is an Executive Committee made up of the senior executive of each partner agency in Ethiopia, or his delegate. The chairmanship will rotate every six months.

4. The JRP has a central Coordination Office headed by a Coordinator responsible to the JRP Executives. Each of the partners will appoint a coordinator and assign responsibilities within their own agency. The coordinators of the partner agencies and the JRP Coordinator will cooperate in all operational and administrative matters.

5. Geographical areas of responsibility: to facilitate the work of the JRP, responsibility for the distribution of the relief food supplies will be share on a geographical basis as follows:

ECS	Eritrea, Tigrai, Assab, Gamo Goffa and Keffa
EECMY/LWF	Wollo, Shoa, Sidamo, Wellega and Ilubabor
EOC	Gondar, Arussi
CRS	Harrarghe, Bale, Gojjam

6. Food Donors — US Government, European Economic Community (EEC), Federal Republic of Germany, Canada, Australia, Italy, Sweden, France and other major donors: In view of the emergency in Ethiopia it is hoped that the terms on which foods are donated will be as broad and flexible as possible. So that there is a uniform system it is agreed that the control accounting and reporting procedures for all food donors be based on the requirements of the US Government as these should more than meet the needs of other donors. Each partner shall:

   (a) make an assessment of their regional food need with periodic monitoring updates,

   (b) facilitate transportation, storage and distribution to NGO operational agencies in their respective regions,

   (c) in accordance with a mutually agreed plan and budget, keep records of distribution, and render accountability to the responsible partner agency so that adequate reports can be forwarded to the appropriate donors.

7. Financing activities:

   (a) each agency will continue to relate to its traditional private funding sources. At the same time, each will attempt to encourage such sources to support the joint effort.

(b) any funds contributed to the individual partners
will remain with the partner unless they wish to
contribute them to the JRP.

(c) all funds obtained for the administration of the JRP
Coordination office will be managed and disbursed
by the JRP coordinator; the JRP shall maintain adequate financial accounts which will be audited at
the discretion of the Executives.

8. Agreements between partner agencies and implementing
agencies responsible for final distribution:

For the JRP Relief Commodities, each partner agency
is required to sign a formal agreement with its implementing agencies responsible for distribution. This spells
out the reporting and accounting responsibilities, and
also requires that they have the distribution approval of
the RRC. Any special arrangements which differ from
the standard should be approved by the Executives.

As the partner agencies of the JRP are responsible
for the distribution of food in their respective regions,
they will be required to make arrangements with the
implementing agencies they will be supplying.

Approved, April 1988

Notes

Numbers in parentheses following individual entries refer to numbered documents in microfilmed archives of the JRP History Project, Catholic Relief Services, Baltimore, Md.

Chapter 1: Raising the Curtain (pages 3–8)

1. Television broadcast, "60 Minutes," CBS, November 18, 1984.
2. Ryszard Kapuscinski, *The Emperor: Downfall of an Autocrat* (New York: Random House, Vintage Books, 1984).
3. Interview with Beth Griffin, New York, July 14, 1988. Unless otherwise indicated, all interviews cited hereafter were conducted by Richard W. and June N. Solberg.
4. Peter Gill, *A Year in the Death of Africa* (London: Paladin Grafton Books, 1986), pp. 4–15; David A. Korn, *Ethiopia, the United States and the Soviet Union* (Carbondale, Ill.: Southern Illinois University Press, 1986), pp. 105–16.

Chapter 2: A Profile of the Land (pages 11–19)

1. Edward Ullendorf, *The Ethiopians: An Introduction to Country and People*, 3d ed. (London: Oxford University Press, 1973), pp. 22–44; Donald M. Levine, *Wax and Gold, Tradition and Innovation in Ethiopian Culture*, Midway reprint ed. (Chicago: University of Chicago Press, 1986).
2. Ullendorf, *The Ethiopians*, pp. 45–92; John Markakis and Nega Ayele, *Class and Revolution in Ethiopia* (Trenton, N.J.: Red

Sea Press, 1986); David A. Korn, *Ethiopia, the United States and the Soviet Union* (Carbondale, Ill.: Southern Illinois University Press, 1986), pp. 1–116.

3. "The Ethiopian Orthodox Church" (2295).

4. "Overview of Ethiopian Catholic Church Activities," May 1986 (1312); Kevin O'Mahoney, *The Ebullient Phoenix: A History of the Vicariate of Abyssinia, 1860–1881*, book 2 (Asmara: Ethiopian Studies Centre, 1987).

5. Gustav Arén, *Evangelical Pioneers in Ethiopia: Origins of the Evangelical Church Mekane Yesus* (Stockholm: EFS Förlaget, 1978); Mercia and E. Theodore Bachmann, *Lutheran Churches in the World* (Minneapolis: Augsburg Fortress, 1989), "Ethiopia."

6. Richard Pankhurst, *The History of Famine and Epidemics in Ethiopia Prior to the Twentieth Century* (Addis Ababa: Relief and Rehabilitation Commission, 1985).

7. *The Challenge of Drought: Ethiopia's Decade of Struggle in Relief and Rehabilitation* (Addis Ababa: RRC, 1985), p. 155.

8. Kurt Jansson, Michael Harris, and Angela Penrose, *The Ethiopian Famine* (London: Zed Books, 1987), pp. 113–18.

Chapter 3: The Impending Disaster (pages 21–32)

1. Kurt Jansson, Michael Harris, and Angela Penrose, *The Ethiopian Famine* (London: Zed Books, 1987), pp. 134–35.

2. Berhe Beyene, "Situation Report about Tigray Administrative Region," September 22–30, 1982 (2327).

3. Abba Stephanos Tedla, "Emergency Situation in Wollo Administrative Region," March 5, 1983 (1851).

4. CRDA Summary of Relief Activities, May 2, 1983 (2695).

5. Interview with Admasu Simeso, Addis Ababa, May 11, 1988; EECMY/LWF/ECE Relief Program in Ethiopia, January to April 1984, p. 9 (2008).

6. Letter, Yacob Tesfai to Brian Neldner, May 3, 1984 (1994).

7. Abba Stephanos Tedla, "Emergency Situation," March 5, 1983 (1851); Peter Gill, *A Year in the Death of Africa* (London: Paladin Grafton Books, 1986), pp. 16–21.

8. Dr. Paul Shears, "Summary Report on Nutritional Situation," April 8, 1983 (2750).

9. Jansson, Harris, and Penrose, *The Ethiopian Famine*, p. 135.

10. Gill, *A Year in the Death of Africa*, pp. 82–88.

11. Interview with Michael Wiest, New York, June 20, 1988.

12. Letter, Geraldine Sicola to David A. Korn, October 14, 1982 (1543).

13. Letter, Thomas Fitzpatrick to Michael Sellers, USAID, Addis Ababa, Supplementary AER for Makelle Emergency Feeding Program, December 7, 1982 (836); report by the U.S. General Accounting Office to the Hon. Byron L. Dorgan, U.S. House of Representatives, "The United States Response to the Ethiopian Food Crisis," April 8, 1985, pp. 14–15.

14. Dorgan Report, p. 15; letter, David Korn to Thomas Fitzpatrick, June 1, 1983 (2411).

15. David A. Korn, Ethiopia, the United States and the Soviet Union (Carbondale, Ill.: Southern Illinois University Press, 1986), p. 52.

16. Letter, Howard Wolpe to Peter McPherson, June 1, 1983, signed by seventy-four congressmen (2410).

17. Washington Post, June 27, 1983.

18. Dorgan Report, pp. 16–17.

19. Interview with Kenneth Hackett by Claire McCurdy, April 27, 1987.

20. Letter, Kenneth Hackett to Richard Solberg, May 11, 1989.

21. Dorgan Report, pp. 17–18.

22. Ibid., p. 19.

23. Letter, Kenneth Hackett to Willard J. Pearson, Washington, D.C., July 20, 1984 (1187).

24. Telex, Rhonda Sarnoff to Kenneth Hackett, July 16, 1984 (1566).

25. Telex, Thomas Fitzpatrick to Kenneth Hackett, July 13, 1984 (1566a).

26. Interview with Thomas Fitzpatrick, Rome, April 18, 1988.

27. Amendment Request for OFDA Emergency Assistance, September 1984 (850).

Chapter 4: Lifelines of Mercy (pages 35–45)

1. Interview with Beth Griffin, New York, July 14, 1988.

2. Interview with John Donnelly, New York, March 1, 1988.

3. CEBEMO, "Euronaid Guidebook for NGOs," July 5, 1986; Dr. Thomas Kerstiens, "E.C. Food Aid — Contributions to Financing the Purchase of Food Products by Non-Government Organiza-

tions," October 21, 1986 (2613); Euronaid, Informative Document: Foreign Aid (Extra-European Community), 1986 (2611).

4. Memorandum on use of LASH barges, CRS/Ethiopia, November 4, 1984 (1591); letter, Catherine Gordon, USAID, to William Rastetter, January 9, 1986 (2443).

5. Interview with Negash Garedew, Addis Ababa, May 6, 1988.

6. Interview with Paavo Faerm, Addis Ababa, May 11, 1988.

7. Draft of Operational Plan for CRS/Ethiopia Emergency Program, January 1, 1985, to June 30, 1986, December 21, 1984, pp. 8–11 (825).

8. Report of the U.N. Office for Emergency Operations in Ethiopia, February 1986 (2509); 1985 Annual Report, LWF/WS Ethiopia Office, December 1985, p. 14 (2004).

9. Cameron Peters, *Logistics Manual I: Warehouse Practice*, April 1986 (1146); Robert Roche, *Logistics Manual II: Commodity Management System*, April 1986 (1147).

10. Telex, Robert Quinlan to Lawrence Pezzullo, October 30, 1984 (508).

11. Dawit Wolde Giorgis, *Red Tears* (Trenton, N.J.: Red Sea Press, 1989), pp. 199, 235–37.

12. Interview with Thomas Fitzpatrick, Rome, April 18, 1988; notes on meeting of EECMY/LWF/CDAA/E Relief Office, May 14, 1985, p. 2.

Chapter 5: The Ecumenical Impulse (pages 47–66)

1. Eugene Ries to Ludwig Geissel, Gunther Hoelter, Nicholas Maro, Robert Quinlan, Georg Specht, February 1, 1984 (2a).

2. Interview with Neil Brenden, Washington, D.C., November 1, 1988.

3. Minutes, meeting of LWS Related Agencies, Geneva, February 14, 1984 (4).

4. Press release, March 15, 1984 (492).

5. Emmanuel Abraham, "The African Drought — An Ecumenical Response," a presentation at a press conference in Geneva, March 15, 1984.

6. Minutes, meeting on African Drought Situation, Geneva, February 15, 1984, p. 4.

7. Minutes, second Coordinating Committee meeting, CDAA, Geneva, April 17, 1984 (10).

8. Minutes, third Coordinating Committee meeting, CDAA, Rome, June 15, 1984 (12).

9. Minutes, meeting on African Drought Situation, Geneva, February 15, 1984, pp. 3-4.

10. Telex, Robert Quinlan to Robert McCloskey, March 15, 1984 (491).

11. Telex, Geraldine Sicola to Kenneth Hackett, July 20, 1984 (1570).

12. Telex, Rhonda Sarnoff to Kenneth Hackett, July 16, 1984 (1566); telex, Geraldine Sicola to Kenneth Hackett, July 20, 1984 (1569).

13. Telex, Geraldine Sicola to Kenneth Hackett, July 20, 1984 (1570).

14. Memorandum from personal file of Leo Siliamaa, October 9, 1984 (2011).

15. Dawit Wolde Giorgis, Red Tears (Trenton, N.J.: Red Sea Press, 1989), p. 153.

16. David A. Korn, Ethiopia, the United States and the Soviet Union (Carbondale, Ill.: Southern Illinois University Press, 1986), p. 121; Washington Post, September 12, 1984.

17. Washington Post, September 18, 1984.

18. September 20, 1984.

19. Telex, Lawrence Pezzullo to Kenneth Hackett, September 20, 1984 (1195).

20. CRDA Appeal to Donor Governments and Agencies, September 28, 1984 (2034).

21. Conversation with Kenneth Hackett, New York, April 13, 1989.

22. Telex, Kenneth Hackett and Michael Wiest to Ken Curtin, October 8, 1984 (1576); interview with Kenneth Hackett by Claire McCurdy, April 24, 1987; conversation with Michael Wiest, New York, April 14, 1989.

23. Conversations with Kenneth Hackett and Michael Wiest, New York, April 13, 1989.

24. Dawit Wolde Giorgis, introductory statement to donors' meeting, Addis Ababa, October 8, 1984, p. 12 (2619); see also Dawit Wolde Giorgis, Red Tears (Trenton, N.J.: Red Sea Press, 1989), p. 179.

25. Conversation with Kenneth Hackett, New York, April 13, 1989; memorandum from Kenneth Hackett to Archbishop Thomas

White, accompanied by a situation report on conditions in Tigray, October 9, 1984 (1577).

26. Telex, Kenneth Hackett/Michael Wiest to Ken Curtin, October 8, 1984 (1576).

27. Telex, Gerhard Meier to Patrice Robineau, October 16, 1984 (1889); press release, CDAA, Geneva, October 30, 1984 (1895).

28. Conversation with Kenneth Hackett, New York, April 13, 1989.

29. Interview with Brian Neldner, Geneva, April 12, 1988.

30. Conversation with Kenneth Hackett, New York, April 13, 1989; conversation with Michael Wiest, New York, April 13, 1989.

31. Minutes, meeting of potential partners, Addis Ababa, October 17, 1984 (42); interview with Peter Lumb, Geneva, April 13–14, 1988.

32. Minutes of smaller group to discuss proposed Joint Famine Relief Program, October 18, 1984 (43); minutes, meeting of agencies participating in Joint NGO Nutrition Intervention Program: Ethiopia Famine Emergency, Addis Ababa, October 22, 1984 (44).

33. Telex, Kenneth Hackett to Brian Neldner, October 25, 1984 (500); conversations with Kenneth Hackett and Michael Wiest, New York, April 14, 1989.

34. Telex, Lawrence Pezzullo to all CRS programs, October 25, 1984 (1334).

35. Telex, Kenneth Hackett to Brian Neldner, October 25, 1984 (505).

36. World Vision press release, transmitted in telex: Robert Quinlan to Lawrence Pezzullo, October 31, 1984 (1414).

37. Thomas Houston, "Statement of Understanding — Drought and Famine Emergency in Ethiopia," October 17, 1984, accompanied by letter of approval: Dawit to Houston, October 15, 1984 (2777).

38. Minutes, fourth Coordinating Committee meeting, CDAA, Geneva, October 29, 1984, p. 9 (16).

39. Memorandum of phone conversation by Kenneth Hackett with Monsignor Robert Coll, November 2, 1984 (1586).

40. Memorandum of Kenneth Hackett, based on phone conversation with Michael Wiest in Addis Ababa, November 1, 1984 (511).

41. Conversation with Michael Wiest, New York, April 13, 1989.

42. "Establishment of Churches Drought Action Africa/Ethiopia:

Aims, Objectives, and Outline of Working Relationship," final draft revised December 2, 1984 (393); see map, p. 67.

Chapter 6: The World Discovers the Ethiopian Famine (pages 69–79)

1. Audio transcript of TV film "The Role of Television Coverage of the Ethiopian Famine, 1984"; Brian Tetley, *Mo: The Story of Mohammed Amin, Front-line Cameraman* (London: Moonstone Books, 1988), pp. 271–73.

2. Interview with Beth Griffin, New York, July 14, 1988.

3. Oxfam, Ethiopia Bulletin #13, October 29, 1984 (2758). Ethiopia Bulletin #14, November 6, 1984 (2759); Graham Hancock, *Ethiopia: The Challenge of Hunger* (London: Victor Gollancz, 1985), pp. 101–8; Peter Gill, *A Year in the Death of Africa* (London: Paladin Grafton Books, 1986), pp. 93–94.

4. Robert Quinlan to Robert McCloskey, November 15, 1984 (2761).

5. Dawit Wolde Giorgis, *Red Tears* (Trenton, N.J.: Red Sea Press, 1989), pp. 190–93.

6. Ibid., pp. 196–97; news release, U.S. embassy, Addis Ababa, November 3, 1984, "U.S.-Ethiopia Agreement for Disaster Assistance to Ethiopian Drought Victims" (2484).

7. Minutes, Ethiopia Emergency Committee, CRS, New York, November 5, 1984 (1211); CRS, New York, Status Update: Ethiopia, November 6, 1984 (1212); Monsignor Robert Coll to Lawrence Pezzullo, November 5, 1984, enclosing briefing paper for McPherson on Nutrition Intervention Program and request for 225,000 tons of emergency food (516, 387, 388).

8. Interview with Peter Lumb, Geneva, April 13–14, 1988. "Churches Drought Action Africa-Ethiopia (CDAA/E)," December 4, 1984 (394).

9. Note on meeting with Terrence Mooney at Canadian embassy, Addis Ababa, November 15, 1984 (1129).

10. Telex, Kenneth Hackett to Lawrence Pezzullo, November 7, 1984 (1213).

11. Telex, Patriarch Tekle Haymanot to General Secretary, WCC, Geneva, October 26, 1984 (521).

12. Letter, Brian Neldner to George Tsetsis, January 7, 1985 (542).

Chapter 7: How the Hungry Were Fed (pages 81–93)

1. Interview with Sr. Maura O'Donahue by Claire McCurdy, Addis Ababa, April 1987.
2. Interview with Rhonda Sarnoff by Claire McCurdy, April 8, 1987; Dr. Carlo Capone, "Integrating Title II Program with Locally Operated Nutrition, Socio-Economic and Humanitarian Activities," Field Bulletin no. 27, March 1, 1977; Dr. Carlo Capone, "Unprocessed Grain Wheat for Emergency Feeding," November 1984 (1016).
3. "Operational Plan for FY 1985 Supplemental AER for Ethiopia," CRS, January 14, 1985, pp. 9–10 (859).
4. Nancy Fronczak and others, "CDAA/E Nutrition Program Guidelines," January 31, 1985 (477).
5. Almaz Fiseha and Nancy Fronczak, "Emergency Food and Nutrition Program (Training Manual)," March 1985, part 1, pp. 1–7 (1148).
6. Interview with Susan Barber, New York, February 5, 1988.
7. "Proposal to OFDA for a Grant Amendment, January 1 through September 30, 1985," January 4, 1985, p. 5 (858).
8. Interview with Susan Barber, New York, February 5, 1988.
9. "Operational Plan for FY 1985," CRS, January 14, 1985, pp. 16–17 (859).
10. Fiseha and Fronczak, "Emergency Food and Nutrition Program (Training Manual)," part 2, p. 6 (1148).
11. Ibid., part 1, pp. 10–12 (1148).
12. Ibid., part 1, pp. 28–30 (1148).
13. "Operational Plan for FY 1985," CRS, January 14, 1985, pp. 17–18 (859); Dr. Hanne Larssen, "Medical Guidelines and Protocol for Emergency Food and Nutrition Program Workers," EECMY Central Office, 1985.
14. EECMY/LWF/ECE Relief Work, Situation and Activity Report, September–December 1984 (2014).
15. Final Disaster Report: The Ethiopian Drought/Famine, Fiscal Years 1985 and 1986, USAID, Addis Ababa, May 1988, pp. 91–94.

Chapter 8: Launching the Partnership (pages 95–105)

1. Brian Neldner to Dieter Frisch, Director General for Development, EEC, November 13, 1984 (2604).

2. Telex, Robert Quinlan to Kenneth Hackett, November 15, 1984 (1479).

3. Telex, Monsignor Robert Coll to Kenneth Hackett, November 17, 1984 (1480).

4. Minutes, first meeting of CDAA/E Executive Committee, November 15, 1984, p. 1 (46).

5. Minutes, CDAA/E coordinators meeting, November 20, 1984 (182).

6. Telex, Robert Quinlan to Lawrence Pezzullo, November 23, 1984 (1484); CDAA/E Administrative Budget: December 1, 1984, to November 30, 1985 (370); Revised CDAA/E Budget: November 1984 to December 1985 (373).

7. Telex, Monsignor Robert Coll to CRS, New York, November 21, 1984 (528); telex, Coll to CRS, New York, November 29, 1984 (530).

8. David A. Korn, quoted on dust cover of Dawit Wolde Giorgis, *Red Tears* (Trenton, N.J.: Red Sea Press, 1989).

9. Notes on meeting with Teunis van Weelie, December 4, 1984 (2285).

10. Report of a mission to Ethiopia by a WCC pastoral team, December 18–23, 1984, p. 4 (2286).

11. Note on meeting with EOC/DICAD, January 29, 1985 (64).

12. Letter, Nico Keulemans to Richard Solberg, June 13, 1989.

13. Nancy Fronczak and others, "CDAA/E Nutrition Program Guidelines," January 1985 (477).

14. Robert W. Roche, *Field Manual for Commodity Management*, May 1, 1985 (1150).

Chapter 9: Streamlining the Structure (pages 107–116)

1. "Statement of Intent" and "Establishment of Churches Drought Action Africa/Ethiopia: Aims, Objectives and Outline of Working Relationship," February 1, 1985 (361); "Agreement" between CRS and EECMY, February 4, 1985 (359).

2. Interview with Francis Carlin, New York, June 23, 1988.

3. Minutes, 13th CDAA/E Executive Committee meeting, February 15, 1985 (72).

4. Outline of study requested by CDAA/E Executive Committee on "CDAA/E Image," February 20, 1985 (71).

5. Telex, Kenneth Hackett to Lawrence Pezzullo, February 19, 1985 (1243).

6. Minutes, CDAA, Geneva, Steering Committee, March 11, 1985 (36).

7. Peter Lumb, "Proposal for Dealing with Present Difficulties in CDAA/E Partnership," March 10, 1985 (616).

8. Notes on 18th meeting of CDAA/E Executive Committee, May 3, 1985 (80a).

9. "EECMY/LWF Position Paper on Future of CDAA/E," prepared for CDAA/E Executive Committee meeting, May 8, 1985 (76).

10. Notes on 19th meeting of CDAA/E Executive Committee, May 8, 1985 (81).

Chapter 10: Keeping the Wheels Turning (pages 119–131)

1. Situation Report, CRS/Ethiopia, April 2, 1985 (1131).

2. CDAA/E Narrative Progress Report, January–March 1985 (466a).

3. CDAA/E Situation Report, June 1–July 10, 1985 (468).

4. Situation Report, CRS/Ethiopia, April 2, 1985 (1131).

5. Interview with Ann Hudacek, Addis Ababa, May 6, 1988; see also Kurt Jansson, Michael Harris, and Angela Penrose, *The Ethiopian Famine* (London: Zed Books, 1987), p. 29.

6. Quoted by Clifford D. May in *New York Times*, May 17, 1985.

7. Report of U.N. Office for Emergency Operations in Ethiopia, February 1986 (2509).

8. CRS Proposal for Truck Leasing, July 9, 1985 (797); Contract: CRS, Contrax Kenya Ltd., and Conrico Overseas Ltd., October 2, 1985 (802).

9. "CRS/AID Relations during the Course of the Ethiopian Relief Effort," June 26, 1985, pp. 3–5 (934).

10. Notes on 18th CDAA/E Executive Committee meeting, May 3, 1985 (80a); notes on 21st CDAA/E Executive Committee meeting, May 29, 1985 (84); minutes of CDAA/E coordinators meeting, February 6, 1985 (144).

11. Letter, John Donnelly to William Pearson, February 11, 1985 (1257).

12. Letter, Julia Chang Bloch to Lawrence Pezzullo, February 12, 1985 (1260).
13. "CRS/AID Relations," June 26, 1985 (934).
14. Letter, Lawrence Pezzullo to Peter McPherson, May 6, 1985 (1275).
15. Memorandum by John Donnelly, May 22, 1985 (1282).
16. Letter, Lawrence Pezzullo to Peter McPherson, May 23, 1985 (1283).
17. Letter, Peter McPherson to Lawrence Pezzullo, May 30, 1985 (2433).
18. Letter, Fred Fischer to Francis Carlin, May 8, 1985 (2432).
19. CRS Ethiopia, annual reports, 1985, 1986.
20. CRS news release, May 8, 1985, "$30 Million Program for Ethiopia" (1783).
21. Letter, John Donnelly to Steven Singer, July 16, 1985 (1297); notes on CRS-AID meeting in Washington, D.C., June 26, 1985 (1296).
22. Letter, Lawrence Pezzullo to Editor, *New York Times*, August 7, 1985 (1301).
23. Krol Report, November 15, 1985.

Chapter 11: Threat to Unity (pages 133-144)

1. CRS/CDAA/E Emergency Proposal, FY 1985, June 19, 1985 (868).
2. Clifford D. May, *New York Times*, June 10, 1985; Kurt Jansson, Michael Harris, and Angela Penrose, *The Ethiopian Famine* (London: Zed Books, 1987), pp. 59–63.
3. Letter, John Donnelly to Thomas H. Reese III, June 17, 1985 (829).
4. Letter, Steven Singer to John Donnelly, June 29, 1985 (2435).
5. Letter, Julia Chang Bloch to Lawrence Pezzullo, August 22, 1985 (2439).
6. Telex, William Schaufele to Terry Kirch, October 21, 1985 (648).
7. Letter, Julia Chang Bloch to Lawrence Pezzullo, September 10, 1985 (2440).
8. "Briefing Paper, Assessment Team, Ethiopia," November 1985, pp. 4–5 (996).

9. Minutes, CDAA/E coordinators meetings, August 14, 21, 1985 (228, 229); notes on 27th CDAA/E Executive Committee meeting, August 16, 1985 (95).

10. Minutes, 27th CDAA/E Executive Committee meeting, August 16, 1985 (96).

11. Memorandum, Joseph Sprunger to Norman Barth, October 14, 1985 (2200); telex, Francis Carlin to William Schaufele, October 18, 1985 (646).

12. Telex, Francis Carlin to William Schaufele, October 18, 1985.

13. Telex, William Schaufele to CRS/Ethiopia, October 22, 1985 (650).

14. Telex, Francis Carlin to William Schaufele, October 22, 1985.

15. Minutes, 28th CDAA/E Executive Committee, October 23, 1985 (98).

16. Minutes, CDAA/E Executive/CRS/LWR Assessment Team meeting, November 20, 1985 (470).

17. Briefing Paper, Ethiopia Assessment Team, November 1985 (471); trip report, Terrence Kirch, "Visit to Ethiopia," December 31, 1985 (1007); *Lutheran World Information Monthly*, December 1985, p. 11 (1999).

Chapter 12: The Partnership Reaffirmed (pages 147–157)

1. Position paper on the 1986 Joint Famine Relief Needs of ECS, EECMY, CRS, LWF, November 20, 1985 (422, 423).

2. Telex, Francis Carlin to CRS, New York, November 22, 1985 (1663).

3. Final Disaster Report, the Ethiopian Drought/Famine, Fiscal Years 1985 and 1986, USAID, Addis Ababa, May 1988, p. 14 (2391).

4. 1985 Annual Report, LWF/WS Ethiopia Office, December 1985, pp. 14–16 (2004).

5. CDAA/E Executive/CRS/LWR Assessment Team meeting, November 20, 1985 (470); 30th CDAA/E Executive Committee meeting, November 27, 1985 (101).

6. "Statement of Intent" and "Terms of Cooperation for the Joint Relief Programme of ECS/EECMY/CRS/LWF Ethiopia: Aims, Objectives, and Outline of Working Relationship," January 16, 1986 (401, 402); see also Appendix for "Profile of JRP," as revised

and approved in April 1988, to include the Ethiopian Orthodox Church (below, pp. 181–184).

7. Minutes, JRP coordinators meeting, January 22, 1986 (244).

8. Agreement between the Provisional Military Government of Ethiopia (RRC) and CRS-USCC, July 15, 1975 (773).

9. Memorandum, Kenneth Hackett to Lawrence Pezzullo, July 30, 1984 (776); telex, Lawrence Pezzullo to Dawit Wolde Giorgis, September 6, 1984 (778); letter, Francis Carlin to Ato Ahmed Ali, June 10, 1985 (782).

10. Minutes, NGOs meeting with Commissioner Dawit Wolde Giorgis, July 19, 1985 (1632); 1985 Annual Report, LWF/WS, Ethiopia Office, December 1985, pp. 18–19 (2004).

11. Telex, Francis Carlin to William Schaufele, October 25, 1985 (1648); memorandum, Terrence Kirch to William Schaufele, October 28, 1985 (783); memorandum, William Schaufele to Francis Carlin, November 21, 1985 (785); General Agreement for Understanding Relief, Rehabilitation, and/or Development Activities in Ethiopia by Catholic Relief Services, November 19, 1985 (786).

12. Dawit Wolde Giorgis, *Red Tears* (Trenton, N.J.: Red Sea Press, 1989), pp. 343–46.

13. David Atwood, "1986 Emergency Food Assessment for Ethiopia," Executive Summary, September 18, 1985 (2497).

14. Letter, Dr. Solomon Gidada, Niels Nikolaisen, Francis Carlin, and Brother Gregory Flynn to Ato Ahmed Ali, January 3, 1986.

15. Telex, Francis Carlin to William Schaufele, January 27, 1986 (1687); letter, Fred Fischer to Francis Carlin, February 4, 1986 (2447).

16. Interview with Francis Carlin, June 23, 1988.

17. Letter, Francis Carlin to Fred Fischer, February 14, 1986 (1695).

18. Memorandum, John Swenson to William Schaufele, February 18, 1986 (1445).

19. Minutes, 37th JRP Executive Committee meeting, February 14, 1986 (107); JRP Notice to All Implementing Agencies, February 15, 1986 (677); notes, 38th JRP Executive Committee meetings, February 26, 1986 (108).

20. Letter, Walter Bollinger to William Schaufele, April 2, 1986 (2451); telex, Brian Neldner to Francis Stephanos, April 16, 1986 (2087); telex, Francis Carlin to William Schaufele, April 23, 1986 (693).

21. Memorandum, by William Schaufele, CRS/AID meeting,

New York, March 10, 1986 (1353); letter, William Schaufele to Richard Gold, March 14, 1986 (1354).

Chapter 13: Ecumenical Journey (pages 159–172)

1. Minutes, 28th CDAA/E Executive Committee meeting, October 23, 1985 (98).

2. Interview with Kevin Delany, Washington, D.C., November 2, 1988.

3. Memorandum, Kevin Delany to Francis Carlin, November 23, 1985 (720); memorandum, Terrence Kirch to John Swenson, December 26, 1985 (724).

4. Biographical data for each participant was supplied by offices of their respective churches or agencies (740–43).

5. Memorandum, Kevin Delany to Lawrence Pezzullo, "Progress Report on Ecumenical Mission for Ethiopian Famine Relief," January 13, 1986 (725); memorandum, Kevin Delany to William Schaufele, Robert McCloskey, and Kenneth Hackett, "Ecumenical Mission Meeting at RRC," January 27, 1986 (726).

6. Telex, Francis Carlin to William Schaufele, February 26, 1986 (750); Delany interview.

7. Delany interview. News Release, CRS/Ethiopia, "Ethiopian Ecumenical Mission," March 3, 1986 (747).

8. Telex, Kevin Delany to CRS/New York, March 4, 1986 (749).

9. Quoted in an article by Chris Watson, in *Catholic New York*, March 13, 1986.

10. Visit to Ottawa by Ethiopian church groups, March 14, 1986 (755); Delany interview.

11. Archbishop Abune Garima, Ato Francis Stephanos, and Cardinal Paulos Tzadua, "Report on Visit of the Ethiopian Ecumenical Mission Abroad," May 12, 1986, pp. 6–8 (768).

12. Minutes of meeting of Ethiopian team visit in Geneva, March 21, 1986 (757); interview with Francis Stephanos, Addis Ababa, May 2, 1988.

13. Archbishop Garima, Francis Stephanos, Cardinal Paulos, "Report," pp. 8–9 (768).

14. Memorandum, Terrence Kirch, discussion of ecumenical visit with Kevin Delany, March 27, 1986 (762).

15. Interview with Francis Stephanos, May 2, 1988.

16. Minutes, JRP Executive Committee meeting, June 4, 1986
(114); letter, Abba Kidane Mariam Ghibray and Ato Francis
Stephanos to Archbishop Dr. Abune Garima, June 24, 1986 (697);
minutes, JRP Executive Committee meeting, July 2, 1986 (117).

Chapter 14: A Continuing Task (pages 175–179)

1. Letter, Francis Carlin to Fred Fischer, April 28, 1986 (1717).
2. Letter, Archbishop Thomas White to Fred Fischer, June 7,
1986 (1726).
3. Donald Crosson, Thomas Kivlan, and Rhonda Sarnoff, "Assessment of Options for the Phase Down of the JRP Program in
Ethiopia," May 1986, p. 38 (473).
4. Interview with Archbishop Dr. Abune Garima, Addis Ababa,
May 3, 1988.

Index ———————————————————————

McCloskey, Robert, 29, 59, 62
MacDonald, David, 167
MacGuire, James, 130, 138
McPherson, Peter, 28, 54, 135, 167
  visit to Ethiopia of, 73, 74, 99,
    123–24
  and inland transport costs,
    126–28, 155–56
Magdalen College, 162
Makeda, Queen of Sheba, 13
Makelle, 4, 57, 58
  starvation camp in, 3, 8, 22, 23,
    55, 73, 75, 92, 95, 159
  relief program for, 27, 28, 44,
    52, 82, 103
marasmus, 92
Marine Transport Service, 41
Massawa, 17, 40, 41, 121, 135
Mauritania, 82
May, Clifford, 121
Médecins sans Frontières, 44, 165
Meier, Gerhard, 49
Mekane Yesus Church, see Ethio-
  pian Evangelical Church
  Mekane Yesus (EECMY)
Melcher, John, 167
Menelik I, 13
Menelik II, 13
Mengistu Haile Mariam, 7, 12, 13,
  28, 53, 121, 160
Mennonite Central Committee, 32
Milan, University of, 162
Miller, Judith, 27, 53
Mohammed, 13
Mondale, Walter, 71
Morris, Frieda, 69, 70
Morris, Jay, 167
Muslim, 14, 15, 23
Mussolini, Benito, 13

Nairobi, 122
Natali, Lorenzo, 169
National Transport Corporation
  (NATRACO), 41, 121–22
Nazareth, 41, 122, 123, 138, 139
NBC, 28, 44, 62, 69–71
Negash Garedew, 41, 43
Neldner, Brian, 49, 50, 60, 61, 62,
  78

Netherlands, 39, 72
  food grants from, 171
  Reformed Church of, 102
New York Times, 27, 53, 121, 130,
  165
New Zealand, 103
Nigeria, 18
Nikolaisen, Niels, 56, 60, 61, 62,
  64, 76–77, 97, 114
  and food request to AID, 139,
    141, 147, 148
Norway, 25
  Norwegian Church Aid, 87
Nutrition Intervention Program, 25,
  32, 36, 74, 103, 108
  beneficiaries of, 5, 90–91, 120,
    148, 177
  distribution network of, 86–88,
    120, 133–34, 148, 155–56
  field operations of, 82–93, 98,
    120
  food losses of, 92–93
  proposal to U.S. government, 86,
    97–99, 150, 153–54

O'Connor, John, 166
O'Donahue, Maura, 81–82, 162
Ogaden Desert, 12
O'Keefe, Augustine, 56, 61, 62, 64
Oromo, 14, 16,
Ottaway, David, 27, 53
Oxfam, 24, 25, 72

Paige, Trevor, 56
Pankhurst, Richard, 17
Paulos Tzadua, Cardinal, 55, 60,
  162, 166
Pearson, William, 124
Pérez de Cuellar, Javier, 167
Peters, Cameron, 43
Pezzullo, Lawrence, 29, 48
  and inland transport costs, 125,
    126–29, 154–56
  and Joint Aid for Ethiopia, 54,
    59–60, 62
Pontifical Urban University, 162
Portland, University of, 71
"Prester John," 11